The Spiral of History Climaxing with Everything Converging Toward the Center

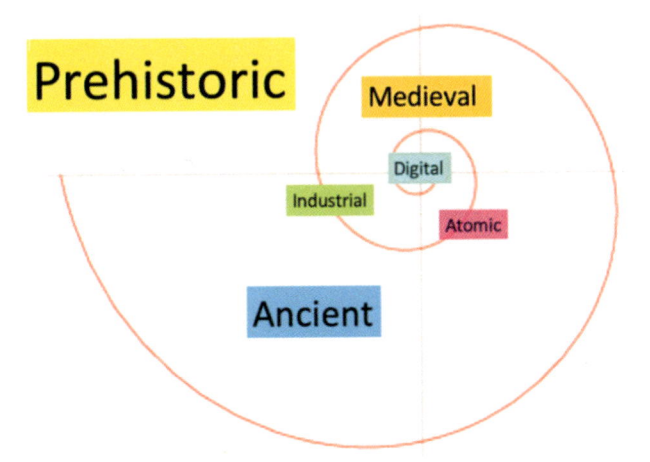

Prehistoric **Medieval** **Digital** **Industrial** **Atomic** **Ancient**

History moves in a spiral or wavelike pattern. There is as marvelous an order and unity to human affairs, including the rise and fall of civilizations, as there is to the helical development of galaxies, solar systems, subatomic particles, DNA, and plants and animals. Today the ages are converging at breakneck speed, and the Spiral, whose roots go back to the origin of our species, is coming to a climax.

At its center, the pace of modern digital life is accelerating, all boundaries are dissolving, and everything is converging. All institutions are breaking down: the family, church, school, hospital, brick-and-mortar store, mall, network and cable TV, even the nation-state. Age-old concepts of race, sex, gender, matter, and spirit are in breathtaking flux.

In the final turn of the Spiral, ultra-processed food, GMOs, bionics, climate change, monocultures, social media, surveillance states, neural networks, gene editing, and coronavirus and other new epidemics are rapidly remaking our world and leading toward an existential crisis between our species and artificial intelligence. An opposite trend, rooted in whole foods and organic agriculture, holistic health and green technology, strives to maintain natural biological and spiritual evolution and create a world of enduring health and peace. *Spiral of History* explores these converging trends and offers insights on how we can avoid impending global catastrophe and create a healthy, peaceful, sustainable future.

Spiral of History

The Arc That Bends Toward Justice, Peace & Love

Book 1. Humanity's Golden Origins
From the Earliest Cookfires
to the Five Peaceful Civilizations

Alex Jack

ΦPLANETARY HEALTH, INC.

Spiral of History
Book 1: Humanity's Golden Origins: From the Earliest Cookfires to the Five Peaceful Civilizations
By Alex Jack

© 2020 by Alex Jack

All rights reserved. Printed in the United States of America.
First Edition

For further information on special sales, mail-order sales, wholesale distribution, translations, foreign rights, contact the publisher: Planetary Health, Inc., Amber Waves Press, PO Box 487, Becket MA 01223, 413-623-0012, planetaryhealth.com

ISBN: 9798618463423

Note on the symbol ϕ on the title page: The Greek letter *phi* (ϕ or φ) is the Golden Mean, the universal proportion of beauty, harmony, and balance. As the number of the logarithmic spiral, *phi* is found throughout nature and art, including the human form, traditional culture, and social dynamics. It also forms the initials of Planetary Health, Inc., the educational nonprofit organization that publishes this book. For more information, please visit www.planetaryhealth.com

IN MEMORY OF MICHIO AND AVELINE KUSHI
AND DEDICATED TO HUMANITY'S COMMON DREAM
OF ONE HEALTHY, PEACEFUL WORLD

"This is a changing world. You will disappear one day, this earth will disappear, and this galaxy will disappear. This visible world will change and its history end. But movement itself—change—is endless, constant, and immortal. Everything in this marvelous universe is changing. The law of change is the key to all questions of peace, happiness, health, and justice. You are a manifestation of God or One Infinity. You change yourself, within infinity, the realm of universal spirit, the eternal dance of yin and yang."—Michio Kushi

Also by Alex Jack

Cooking
Amber Waves of Grain (with Gale Jack)
Complete Guide to Macrobiotic Cooking (with Aveline Kushi)
One Peaceful World Cookbook (with Sachi Kato)

Health & Healing
The Cancer Prevention Diet (with Michio Kushi)
Diet for a Strong Heart (with Michio Kushi)
Basic Home Remedies
Food Governs Your Destiny: The Teachings of Namboku Mizuno (with Aveline Kushi)
AIDS & Beyond (with Michio Kushi)
Humanity at the Crossroads
The Mozart Effect: Tapping the Power of Music to Heal the Body, Strengthen the Mind, and Unlock the Creative Spirit (for Don Campbell)
The Macrobiotic Path (with Michio Kushi)
Chewing Made Easy (with Gale Jack)
Diabetes: A Whole-Foods, Plant-Based Approach (with Bettina Zumdick and Edward Esko)

History & Biography
One Peaceful World (with Michio Kushi)
Aveline: The Story of the Woman Behind Macrobiotics (with Aveline Kushi)
Profiles in Oriental Diagnosis:
  Book 1. The Renaissance
  Book 2. Vegetarian Bride of Frankenstein
  Book 3. Evolution at the Dinner Table
Homer's Odyssey: My Quest for Peace and Justice (for Dr. Homer A. Jack)
The Circle of the Dance: Achilles' Shield, Odysseus's Oar, Calypso's Axe and the New Golden Age

Philosophy & Science
The Book of Macrobiotics (with Michio Kushi)
Let Food Be Thy Medicine
Imagine a World Without Monarch Butterflies (with a forward by Dennis Kucinich)
Biowisdom
Cool Fusion (with Edward Esko)
Corking the Nuclear Genie (with Edward Esko)
Awned, the New Organic

Spiritual Development
The New Age Dictionary
The Gospel of Peace: Jesus's Teachings of Eternal Truth (with Michio Kushi)
A Visit to the Land of the Gods
Buddha Standard Time (for Lama Surya Das)
Diagnosing Dante

Literature & Criticism
Hamlet by Christopher Marlowe and William Shakespeare
As You Like It by Christopher Marlowe and William Shakespeare

Fiction
The Adamantine Sherlock Holmes: The Adventures in India & Tibet
Dragon Brood: A Play on the Vietnam War
Out of Thin Air: A Satire on Grains & Global Warming
Inspector Ginkgo Tips His Hat to Sherlock Holmes

Contents

Front Cover Illustrations — 8

Keywords & Concepts — 9

Overture — 15

1. First Movement: The Spiral of History — 20

2. Second Movement: The Golden Spiral — 43

3. Third Movement: Prehistory — 57

4. Fourth Movement: The Five Peaceful Civilizations — 83

Coda 1: The New Era of Humanity: From 2040 to 2100 — 118

Coda 2: Animals That Cook: Proto-Cooking by Mammals, Birds, Mollusks, & Insects — 122

Coda 3: Prayers, Meditation, and Visualizations by Michio Kushi — 124

Resources — 127

Notes — 128

Index — 135

About the Author — 142

FRONT COVER ILLUSTRATIONS

The Spiral of History is portrayed as a contracting spiral moving centripetally inward from the periphery to the center from the prehistoric era roughly 15,000 or more years ago to about 2030 to 2040 and beyond. The iconic images beginning at the top left generally follow chronological order as they unfold counterclockwise toward the center. However, a few (e.g., Nuclear Power and Dr. Martin Luther King, Jr. and Greta Thunberg) are clustered around the two poles: Rule by Power (lower left) and Advance by by Idea (top right) showing smaller, fractal spirals branching off the main arabesque.

1. Tree of Life (Shaker)
2. Awned wheat (originally from Anatolia)
3. Venus of Willendorf (Austria
4. Bronze sculpture of a farmer and ox plowing a field (Sumer)
5. Statue of Gilgamesh (Uruk)
6. Stonehenge (Ancient Britain)
7. Ma'at, Goddess of Truth (Egypt)
8. *Creation of Adam* by Michelangelo (Renaissance)
9. Nuclear power plants (worldwide)
10. Pyramids at Gizeh (Egypt)
11. Trireme
12. Moses & the Ten Commandments (Ancient Israel)
13. Sarvasati, Hindu Goddess of Learning (India)
14. Rainbow Serpent (Aboriginal Australia)
15. Michio Kushi, praying
16. Krishna playing flute (India)
17. Mayan pyramid at Chichen Itza (Yucatan)
18. Jesus mosaic (Byzantium)
19. Calligraphy with Mohammad's name (Arabia)
20. Antelope mask of Tjiwara, God of Agriculture (Mali)
21. Statue of Guanyin, Bodhisattva of Compassion (China)
22. Kokopelli (American Southwest)
23. Hildegard of Bingen (Rhineland)
24. Dante and the *Divine Comedy* by Domenico di Michelino (Florence)
25. Parzival, Knight of the Holy Grail (Germany)
26. Inka pottery head (Peru)
27. Christopher Marlowe portrait (England)
28. *Mona Lisa* by Leonardo da Vinci (Florence)
29. Taj Mahal (India)
30. Locomotive (worldwide)
31. Sojourner Truth (America)
32. Albert Einstein (Germany)
33. Early biplane (America)
34. Model T automobile (America)
35. First human on the moon (America)
36. Hamburger (worldwide)
37. Dr. Martin Luther King, Jr. (America)
38. Laptop computer (worldwide)
39. iPhone (US, China, worldwide)
40. Greta Thunberg (planet earth)
41. Awned grain (worldwide)

Keywords & Concepts

Ages of Humanity eras of declining virtue, morality, and spiritual wisdom in ancient Greek, Roman, and Hindu mythology, including the Golden, Silver, Bronze/Heroic, and Iron Ages. Mesoamerican creation stories describe five worlds or "Suns" that rise or fall according to human morality and the whims of the gods

Awns are the long, thin hairs extending from the heads of cereal grains growing in the field. Like antennae, they gather and absorb the waves and vibrations of the cosmos, including the sun, moon, stars, and distant galaxies. Eating heirloom barley, wheat, rice, and other awned grains strengthens the will, enhances intuition, and attunes to universal awareness

Chakra (from the Sanskrit "wheel") one of several major energetic centers of the human organism, extending from the crown of the head to the root of the spine and including the "third eye" (associated with the pineal gland), throat, heart, navel, and small intestine. The chakras connect to the **meridians**, an invisible branching network that channels natural electromagnetic energy (*Qi*) to the organs and functions, cells and tissues

Civilization in this book refers to large, complex societies and does not imply moral or spiritual superiority. They may or may not include central authority, domestication of plants and animals, specialization of labor, monumental architecture, taxation, temple worship, and other hallmarks. Indeed, most indigenous or "primitive" people were more egalitarian, democratic, and peaceful than "civilized" societies that treated them as "barbarians" and "uncivilized"

Cline gradual gradient of a species across a geographical range. *Cline* is now the preferred term among anthropologists instead of *race*, which is considered illusory and unscientific

Divine Feminine is the dimension of the self, nature, and the cosmos associated with nurturing, intuition, cooperation, compassion, and community. In the pre-historic world, it manifested as the Great Goddess, Mother Nature, yin energy, and other largely impersonal forces. In the historical era, it was also revered in the personification of Isis, Asherah, Virgin Mary, Radha, Kuan Yin, Ix Chel, and other female deities and personages

Epigenetics the study of changes in DNA resulting from diet, environment, lifestyle, peak or traumatic experiences, and other factors that can be passed on to offspring

Five Peaceful Civilizations refer to the ancient Minoans in the Aegean, Indus Sarasvati Civilization in Pakistan and India, Niger River Valley

Civilization in West Africa, Norte Chico Civilization in South America, and the Ancestral Australians that all had complex societies that endured harmoniously for a thousand years or more. They were egalitarian, honored the feminine divine, ate awned grains as principal food, and had naturalistic art and culture. They also had writing or a symbolic communication system. They had virtually no hierarchy, patriarchy, religion, or war and are largely missing from contemporary history books

Fractals are objects in which the same patterns occur again and again at different scales and sizes. In nature, these spiral forms include branching plants (broccoli, okra, ferns), neurons, crystal growth, fluid turbulence, and galaxy formation

Gatherer-Hunters traditional foragers whose food consisted predominantly of wild plants (ca. 80–85%) and a small amount of game, fish, or other animal fare (ca. 15–20%); a term preferred by some anthropologists to counter the stereotypical image of "man the hunter"

Gondwanan and Lurasian ancient mythologies dating to ca. 50,000 years ago. The Gondwanan, still found in Africa, Australian, and other Southern climes, revolves around a peaceful creator, plant-based diet, and vegetative myths. The Lurasian spans Europe, Asia, and much of the Americas and centers on fearsome deities, a heavenly hierarchy and earthly dynasties, the hero's quest, slaying of a dragon or other monster, and significant animal food consumption

Golden Ratio a proportion approximating 0.618... that appears in many patterns in nature, including the spiral arrangement of leaves, petals, and other plant parts, as well as ratios in the body (e.g., head to torso), weather patterns, financial forecasts, social dynamics, and other phenomena. The traditional standard of beauty, harmony, and balance

Homo (Latin for "human") is the genus that emerged with *Australopithecus* and includes *Erectus*, *Neanderthals*, *Denisovans*, and *Sapiens*. **Hominids** is a broad taxonomic family of primates including orangutans, gorillas, chimpanzees, bonobos, and humans. **Hominins** includes all evolutionary lines of humans

Logarithmic Spiral a long, graceful self-replicating arc that appears throughout nature and reveals the mechanism of creation and the fundamental unity and interconnectedness of life. Galaxies, solar systems, and subatomic particles manifest it. Birds and animals, flowers and trees, and all other flora and fauna observe its laws. The growth and development of families, companies, cities, nations, and other social phenomena also reflect its dynamics

Precession of the Equinoxes an astronomical cycle of 25,800 years in which the wobble of the earth on its axis causes the North Star to change every several thousand years. The end of the current cycle, governed by Polaris, will end about 2100 CE. Known traditionally as the Platonic or Great Year, scientists and astrologers interpret it very differently

Qi Energy natural electromagnetic energy of the universe streaming from heaven and earth, animating all things, coursing through meridians and chakras, activating cells and tissues, organs, systems, and functions. Also known as *Ki* (Japan), *prana* (India), *nyama* (West Africa), *ruach* (ancient Israel), *oreda* (Iroquois), *arunquiltha* (Australia), Holy Spirit (Christianity), etc. Qi is the Chinese term, best known in *taiqi* (old spelling *tai ch'i*)

Spiral of History the logarithmic pulse of history and social change from the worldwide rise of city-states in about 3200 BCE to the globalized world of the 2030s, encompassing the agricultural, industrial, and digital revolutions

Tjiwara the divine, half-human, half-antelope culture bearer of West Africa who introduced brown rice cultivation and other arts and sciences to humans in antiquity. A traditional mask of Tjiwara inspired young Picasso to literally change the face of modern art, giving rise to Cubism and other new nonrepresentational forms of perception

Traditional Diet of Humanity the way of eating that originated about 4 million years ago when primates started to eat wild sorghum, rice, millet, and teff. These awned grains were complemented with sedges, roots, leaves, steams, fruits, seeds, nuts, honey, water, and other natural foods, including small amounts of wild game, fish, and other animal quality food. With the mastery of fire about 2 million years ago, cooking spurred neurological development, leading to tool use, language, art, and other cultural advances

Yin and Yang the law of universal change; the forces and tendencies that differentiate from the infinite universe or the divine (God, Allah, Dao, Supreme Buddha) and manifest as spirit and matter, centrifugal and centripetal energy, and space and time. Yin and yang are the origin of all relative worlds and appear as complementary opposites, including expansion and contraction, above and below, female and male, rest and movement, vertical and horizontal, etc. All phenomena include both yin and yang qualities in various proportions, and these two forces constantly transform into each other. None is fixed or absolute. Yin and yang reflect the Golden Ratio and are also known as the **Unifying Principle**

Spiral of History

Achilles's Shield in Homer's *Iliad* depicts the Golden and Silver Ages,
the Bronze and Iron Ages, and the coming New Golden Age,
spiraling from heaven and earth in the center
(from *The Homer Encyclopedia*)

BOOK 1. HUMANITY'S GOLDEN ORIGINS:
FROM THE EARLIEST COOKFIRES
TO THE FIVE PEACEFUL CIVILIZATIONS

"History never repeats itself, but it often does rhyme."
—Mark Twain

*I am food, I am the eater of food.
Who knows this, knows.*
—Upanishads, 6th century BCE

*"Whether you have feet, wings, fins, or roots,
we are all in it together."*
—Winona LaDuke

OVERTURE

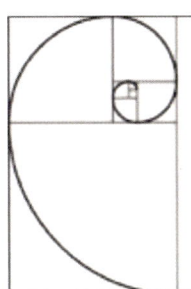

Life moves in a spiral, and spirals are among the earliest forms of art around the world (see Figure 1). There is as marvelous an order and unity to history and human affairs, including the rise and fall of cultures and civilizations, as there is to the helical development of galaxies, solar systems, subatomic particles, DNA, and plants and animals. The Spiral of History (see the front cover and Figures 5 and 6 in the next chapter) can be divided into twelve sections like a clock. But because of the logarithmic nature of the spiral, the "hours" or ages are not equal in size or duration but like a chambered nautilus trace a graceful curve.

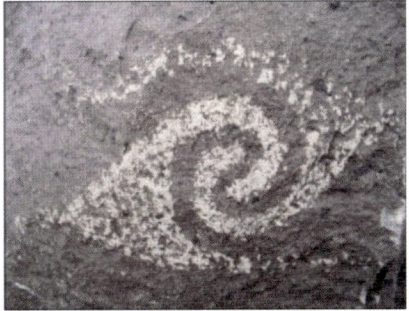

Figure 1. Rock art from France ca. 20,000 years ago (left) shows humans singing and dancing with the animals. Note how the composition forms a rough spiral from the central figure playing a flute moving outward. Native American spiral petroglyph (right)

History actually does repeat itself to an extent, or rhymes as Mark Twain reputedly put it. For example, the Crusades and the Mongol invasions of the Middle Ages fall in the same section as the World Wars in the modern era. The European discovery and exploration of the Western Hemisphere prefigured space exploration and the race to the moon between the superpowers during the Cold War. The quality of each section is the same; the main difference is that in the past, the pace of life was slower, and each era lasted longer. Today, the ages are converging at breakneck speed, and the whole spiral, spanning the entire existence of our species, is coming to a climax.

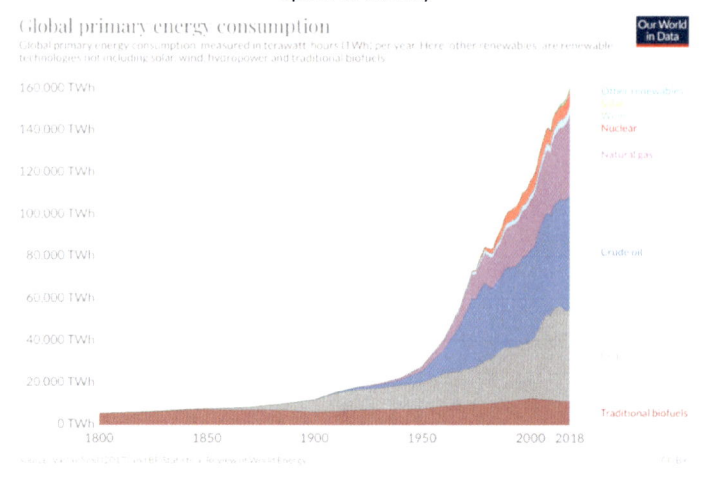

Figure 2. Global primary energy consumption, measured in terawatt-hours (TWh) per year, follows a logarithmic progression going back to antiquity. Traditional biofuels (bottom) include wood and charcoal

As an illustration of the logarithmic advance of civilization, take fire. Its use for cooking, warmth, and energy has increased at an exponential rate with each new source of fuel taking about one third as long to develop as the previous stage. Fire's domestic, metallurgical, and other pyro-technological application changed from wood to charcoal after about three thousand years of recorded history. Then from charcoal to coal took another thousand years. From coal to petroleum about three hundred years went by. From petroleum and natural gas to fossil fuel-generated electricity less than a century passed, and from electric to nuclear another thirty years transpired (see Figure 2).

Spiral of History explores the logarithmic and fractal (or self-replicating) nature of human life, culture, and society and offers a revolutionary new paradigm of humanity's origin and destiny. Like *Sapiens: A Brief History of Humankind* by Yuval Noah Harari, *Behave: The Biology of Humans at Our Best and Worst* by Robert Sapolsky, David Reich's *Who We Are and How We Got Here: Ancient DNA and the New Science of the Human Past*, and other recent books that fundamentally challenge our assumptions about culture and society, *Spiral of History* offers a novel approach to our species' origin and destiny.

After thousands of years, the long, winding logarithmic Spiral of History is now cresting. Viewed as an inward moving centripetal curve, we are now moving through the very center of the Spiral. The pace of modern life is accelerating rapidly, all boundaries are dissolving, and everything is converging. All familiar institutions are breaking down: the family, church, school, hospital, brick-and-mortar store, union, and even the nation-state. Age-old concepts of race, sex, gender, matter, and spirit are in breathtaking flux.

In the final revolution of the Spiral, fast food, bionics, climate change, monocultures, GMOs, digital empires, gene editing, and virtual and augmented realities are rapidly remaking our world and leading toward an existential climax between our species and artificial intelligence (AI). Self-replicating algorithms and neural networks are displacing human beings in transportation, communications, finance, law, medicine, and many other domains. A complementary opposite trend, rooted in whole foods and organic agriculture, integrative medicine, green technology, and meditation and mindfulness techniques, strives to maintain natural biological and spiritual evolution, pass safely through this cataclysmic time, and create a sustainable future.

Which of these tendencies will prevail? Or as depicted in contemporary science fiction, art, and animation, will some cyborg species or hybrid society emerge? Regardless of what path our species takes, there is always the danger that the world as we know it will self-destruct through nuclear accident or war, global warming and climate change, pandemic disease, cyber war, or another apocalypse. If the past is prologue, our history over the last five thousand years is not very sanguine. For untold individuals, families, communities, and nations, life was filled with unspeakable evil, unbearable suffering, and endless anguish. At a personal level, the human condition has been accompanied by accident, illness, the loss of a child, parent, partner, or beloved animal companion. Failure in love, career, or other domain has also been the lot of many. As James Joyce lamented, "History is a nightmare from which I am trying to awake."[1] For countless others, life has been accompanied by inexpressible joy, ineffable beauty, and abiding love.

Such is the paradox of human life. On balance, as Christianity, Hinduism, Buddhism, and many other great historical faiths hold, this world is a vale of tears, and suffering and ultimate deliverance can only be realized in another realm. Yet as Martin Luther King, Jr. reminds us, "The arc of the moral universe is long, but it bends toward justice."[2] This sentiment was originally enunciated by Theodore Parker, a Unitarian minister and Abolitionist leader in Boston in the Civil War era. It was widely admired and popularized by Dr. King. Although an evangelical Christian minister, he was an admirer of the Declaration of Independence, an imperfect proclamation beginning with the immortal phrase "all men [and women] are created equal." He also upheld an even more imperfect document, the U.S. Constitution, that had originally counted enslaved African Americans as only three-quarters human for determining state representation. But Dr. King believed in the perfectibility of human society and strove to create a more perfect union. He was also an adherent of the Social Gospel, a movement in Protestantism that applied Christian ethics to the problems of society. As the leader of the modern civil rights movement, he successfully utilized Gandhian methods of nonviolent direct action to effect peaceful change.

Our reading of history largely shares the view that humanity can surmount its history and create a healthy, egalitarian, and compassionate society. This conviction is central to all the world's great religious and spiritual teachers, if not always the religions and other institutions that grew up around them. In the last chapter of this book, we will focus on what I call the

Five Peaceful Civilizations. These are complex societies in Europe, Pakistan-India, Africa, South America, and Australia that each flourished for more than a thousand years without central government, religion, violence, or war. These remarkable cultures—the Minoan, Indus-Sarvasati Valley, Niger River Valley, Norte Chico, and Ancestral Aboriginal—were devoted to nature, art, and trade and had sophisticated sciences and technologies. Several have only been discovered in recent decades, and virtually all are missing from school textbooks. Instead, we are led to believe that civilization began in Sumer, Egypt, China, Vedic India, ancient Israel, Greece, Rome, and pre-Columbian America. For all too long, we have assumed that monarchy and temple worship, the subordination of females, the division of rich and poor, slavery, bloodshed and war, and environmental destruction are natural and inevitable. Clearly, these well-known historic civilizations in the Fertile Crescent and elsewhere are the seed of today's polarized and fractured world, but there is nothing inevitable about the extremes they embodied and bequeathed us.

Figure 3. Paul Gaugin's *Where Do We Come From? What Are We? Where Are We Going?* (1897)

Despite this tragic legacy of oppression and war, prejudice and discrimination, the Spiral of History bends toward justice, peace, and love—the values that largely prevailed in human prehistory, the Five Peaceful Civilizations they displaced, and among prophets and visionaries who emerged in East and West, North and South, over the last five thousand years. Drawing on the vast panorama of human art and culture, science and civilization, *Spiral of History* will explore these contrasting and diverging trends. In the spirit of Gauguin's reflective Tahitian painting, *Where Do We Come From? What Are We? and Where Are We Going?* (see Figure 3), we will explore our heritage as a planetary family. We will also add several more queries, *Where Did We Go Wrong?* and *What Can We Do About It?* At the climax of our journey, we will look at what the future holds and how we can avoid worldwide disaster and create a healthy, joyful, and sustainable future.

Spiral of History will appeal to parents, children, and other family members, as well as historians, scientists, nurses and physicians, environmentalists, artists, cooks, librarians, workers, farmers, and everyone trying to make sense of the world we live in and the bewildering pace of modern change. It will help illuminate the polarizing trends that are rapidly converging today. From the personal to the social, the natural to the cybernetic, the visionary to the practical, *Spiral of History* will present a sweeping new model of history that rediscovers and celebrates our true peaceful human origins and the largely harmonious and joyful early chronicle of our species. It will explain the dynamic forces that shape and influence human affairs and satisfy the quest for deeper purpose and meaning to life and history. The book will identify the evolutionary crossroads humanity now faces and glance at the radically different quantum futures that lie ahead. We will offer simple, commonsense guidelines for individuals, families, companies, communities, nations, and global networks to pass safely through this at once perilous and glorious time.

While narrative order is important in synethesizing and presenting content, aesthetic function also enhances the experience of the whole. The book is structured on the metaphor of a symphony, starting with an overture (preface), four movements (chapters), and several codas (appendices). The result is not as fractal as I would have liked, but like vines, petals, and leaves, it is a start at composing an organic, plant-rich chronicle of our species' history.

I am grateful to my parents Homer and Esther and my grandparents David Rhys Williams, Lucy Adams Williams, Alexander Jack, and Cecelia Davis Hecht, who ignited my passion at an early age for peace and justice, as well as past generations of ancestors, some of whose lives have come alive for me in family history. I am deeply appreciative of Michio and Aveline Kushi, Franklin Myers, Ernest Painter, Paul and Gail Schmidt, J. Krishnamurti, Thich Tri Quang, Joseph Campbell, Ms. Shen Nyorai, and other beloved teachers and mentors through the years who opened new avenues of perception for me in the fields of cosmology, mythology, history, spiritual development, and the health of society. I am also thankful for the love and support of my daughter Mariya and her family; my sister Lucy and her family; Ann Fawcett, Barbara Gale Fields, and other significant others; and many friends, colleagues, and students for their insights and suggestions. Bettina Zumdick, Sachi Kato, Nadine Barner, Blake Alcott, Anne Teresa de Keersmacher, Wieke Nelissen, and other close friends commented on some of this material, and I am grateful for their reflections and encouragement. Finally, I am grateful for Mischa, my beautiful golden cat with the long awned whiskers, who loved to drape himself on my lap (and frequently laptop) while I composed this book.

Because of its breadth and scope, *Spiral of History* is conceived as a multivolume work. Following Book 1, other books in the series will cover the ancient and medieval worlds, the modern world, and the unfolding digital and sustainable worlds. Further information on this project, and on related publishing and teaching activities, is available at www.planetaryhealth.com.

Alex Jack
The Berkshires
February 4, 2020

1
SPIRAL OF HISTORY

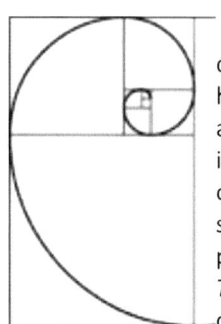

The universe has often been compared to a giant clock. Thinkers in the early modern era likened God to a heavenly watchmaker. In the view of Newton, Descartes, and the Deists, the creator set the world in motion, winding up the cosmic clock, and then left it to operate on its own according to the mechanical laws of nature. Many scientists today find no need to bring the Deity into the process. As the title of Richard Dawkins' bestselling book, *The Blind Watchmaker*, suggests, the purposeless, random laws of physics and biology are sufficient to account for all of matter and life. The Big Bang, planetary science, natural selection, and genetics, according to this view, can explain the origin of our planet and its myriad life forms.

As a child, the Doomsday Clock loomed large in my imagination. According to the *Bulletin of the Atomic Scientists*, a publication to which my father, Dr. Homer A. Jack, a Unitarian minister and social activist, contributed as executive director of SANE, the major peace and disarmament group during the Cold War, the world was on the brink of nuclear annihilation. The Doomsday Clock was originally set at 7 minutes before midnight. Since then it has been reset periodically, most recently in January, 2020 to 100 seconds until midnight—the closest ever—as resurgent nationalism, the slow-motion resumption of the arms race between America and Russia, the nuclear soliloquizing of North Korea, cyber warfare, unregulated genetic engineering, hypersonic weapony, and the inexorable warming of the earth, gravely imperil the future of our planet.

Then there are the ages of humanity to consider: the ancient world; the medieval world, and the modern world. Each in turn is divided into sub periods such as the Paleolithic, the Mesolithic, and the Neolithic; the early middle ages, the high middle ages, the late middle ages; the early modern world, the late modern world, and the post-modern world. In ancient Greece, the Four Ages of Humanity reflected eras of declining virtue, peace, and prosperity, starting with the paradisiacal Golden Age, followed by the tarnished Silver Age, the brutal Bronze Age and Age of Heroes, and ending with the oppressive and immoral Iron Age. In Vedic India, there were also Four Ages, mirroring a similar spiritual and moral lapse, culminating in the present Kali Yuga.

The Aztec, Maya, and other Mesoamerican cultures believed in successive Suns, or worlds, that came into being, flourished, and were destroyed by heaven-sent catastrophes. We are now said to be near the end of the Fifth Sun. According to a centuries-old Hopi Prophecy, a "gourd of ashes" would be invented and, if dropped from the sky, boil the oceans and burn the land, causing nothing to grow for many years. At the end of World War II, this peaceful Native American tribe in the desert Southwest interpreted this prophecy as the atomic bombing of Hiroshima and Nagasaki. The final stage of the Hopis' visionary predictions—the Great Day of Purification—will culminate in either the total rebirth of life on the planet or its annihilation.[3] In Western astrology, the dawn of the Age of Aquarius signifies the return of a golden age of love and peace. Among historians and scientists today, a popular classification is the *anthropocene*, an epoch spanning from about 15,000 BCE to the present during which our species has significantly impacted the earth's geology, habitats, and climate, especially through fossil fuel use.

For the most part, there is no unifying principle governing when one age or era begins and ends and their relation to each other. They follow sequentially one after another, in most cases linearly and in a few circularly. Throughout history, it has been commonly observed that the pace of life has gradually increased, and humanity has made steady material and technological progress—often inversely proportional to moral and spiritual improvement. But there hasn't been a widespread recognition that history itself obeys the same laws as the distribution of elements, the motions of planets, and the evolution of plants and animals.

Figure 4. Educator Michio Kushi lecturing on the Spiral of History in Boston in the early 1970s

Educator Michio Kushi was the first to discern the spiral nature of historical events—whether on a personal, social, planetary, or epochal scale. Though best known as the leader of the international macrobiotic community, father of the modern natural foods movement, and a dietary and way of life counselor who aided thousands of people to heal themselves of cancer, heart disease, diabetes, and many other chronic disorders, Michio was a universal thinker and spiritual guide. Following studies in international law and political science at Tokyo University and Columbia University, he immersed himself in cosmic and biological evolution as well as the unfolding pageant of human life. Like Jesus, Buddha, Swedenborg, Toynbee, Joseph Needham, George Ohsawa, and other spiritual teachers and historians he admired, he strived to discern the pattern underlying humanity's material and spiritual origin and destiny. Beginning with lectures at the Arlington Street Unitarian Church in Boston in the late 1960s (see Figure 4) and climaxing with the creation of the Michio Kushi Permanent Collection at the Smithsonian's Natural Museum of American History in 1998 at the turn of the millennium, Michio and his wife and teaching partner, Aveline, taught Order of the Universe studies (spanning cosmology, philosophy, and science) and introduced the Spiral of History as a paradigm to understand the pulse of human development and social change. Using yin and yang, the complementary opposite tendencies in Far Eastern philosophy and medicine, as a compass, Michio taught that cosmic and terrestrial evolution can be understood as a dynamic movement from contraction and materialization to expansion and spiritualization. In each stage, he explained, there is a logarithmic relationship in which *yin*, or expansive energy, stands in a dynamic ratio to *yang*, or contractive energy.

His model of history bears some affinity with the twelve-spoked wheel of time in Indian thought that measures world ages in alternating ascending and descending arcs. But the Hindu and Buddhist versions tend to have recurring cycles with fixed periods, while Michio's is spirallic and dynamic or flexible.

Michio's original diagram illustrated the first two revolutions, or full turns, of the Spiral from about 3200 BCE until the Space Age in the 1960s. Over several decades in New England, as editor-in-chief of *East West Journal* and director of the Kushi Institute and the One Peaceful World Society, I worked with him closely on many educational, medical research, and healing projects. We wrote a dozen books together, and for *One Peaceful World* (1986) we mapped the contours of the third and concluding revolution of the Spiral, spanning 1980 to the 2040s and beyond. Figure 5 is a modified version of that illustration, showing a contracting spiral winding into the center until 2040. For this book, I have further changed and simplified some of the labels and given names to the three broad orbits (The Agricultural Revolution, The Industrial Revolution, and The Digital Revolution), but it is essentially the same. See Coda 1 and Figure 76 for the original diagrams of the two broad quantum futures opening up.

Spiral of History 23

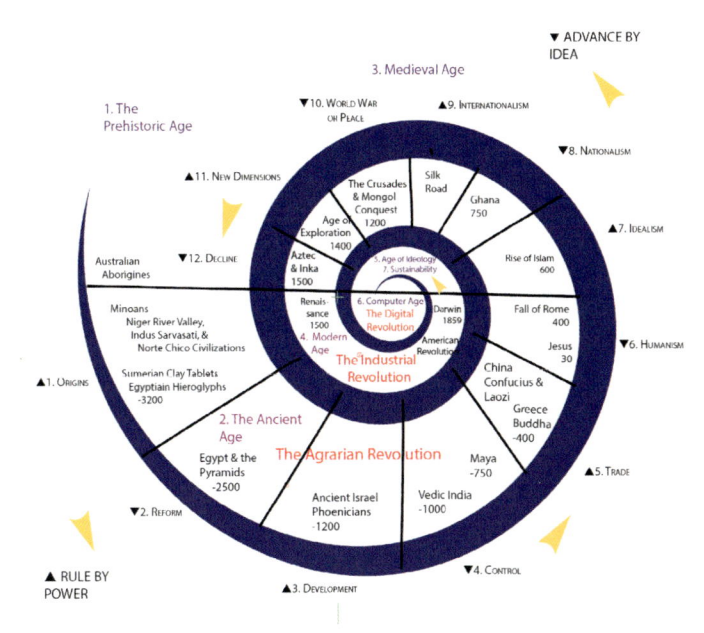

Figure 5. YANG VIEW: The Spiral of History begins about 3200 BCE and winds counterclockwise into the center until about 2040

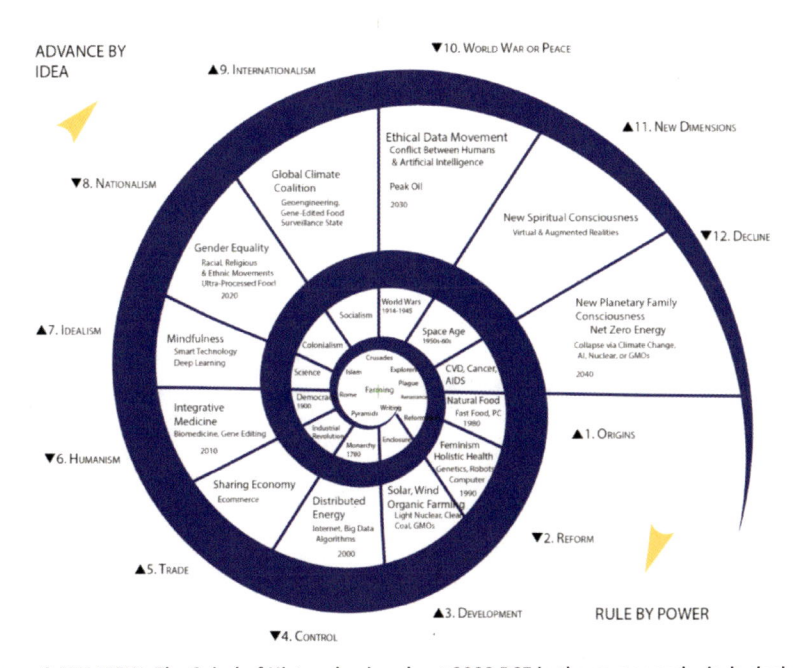

Figure 6. YIN VIEW: The Spiral of History begins about 3200 BCE in the center and winds clockwise to the periphery to 2040 and beyond

Twin Perspectives

In the Paleolithic era, the pace of life remained relatively unchanged for many eons up until historic times. With the spread of farming, the advent of writing, and urbanization, life gradually began to speed up. Still, ancient civilizations, such as the Egyptian and Chinese, were relatively slow and long lived, often lasting thousands of years, while medieval empires and kingdoms spanned centuries. In the present era, nation-states, geopolitical blocs, and multinational corporations—the bodies that exert real governance today—commonly last for only decades and, in the case of digital dynasties, often a matter of years.

Michio's original Spiral of History diagram depicts a contracting (or yang) spiral moving from the periphery to the center. It shows the length of each age shrinking as it coils inward toward the middle. To complement Michio's original Spiral of History, I have created another graphic for this book showing an expanding (or yin) spiral moving in the opposite direction from the center to the periphery (see Figure 6). The illustration looks at the process from an energetic or spiritual view. The first, more yang Spiral diagram offers a structural view, the second, more yin Spiral a functional view.

The two Spiral diagrams show how history unfolds from complementary opposite views. In the contracting Spiral (see Figure 7, *left*), in Vector 1 Origins, representing the beginning of historical civilization, *Farming/Writing* occupies a relatively large section in the peripheral, outermost curve (about 8 to 9 o'clock), Chemical *Farming/Printing* in the middle section, and *Organic Farming/GMOs/Texting* a tiny section in the innermost curve in the center (also about 8 to 9 o'clock).

Figure 7. Detail of Vector 1 *Origins* in the contracting Spiral (*left*) and in the expanding Spiral (*right*)

In the expanding Spiral (see Figure 7, *right*), the *Farming/Writing* revolution in Vector 1 Origins is located in the small inner turn of the spiral (about 3 to 4 o'clock), while *Chemical Farming/Printing* occupies the middle section and *Organic Farming/GMOs/Texting* occupies a larger section in the last outer turn of the spiral (also about 3 to 4 o'clock). This expanding yin spiral shows consciousness expanding with each era and the impact of unfolding events growing and influencing successively larger domains of thought and vibration.

In Far Eastern philosophy, yin and yang are not fixed, but dynamic tendencies, constantly changing one into another. Yin and yang have no meaning in isolation, only in relation to each other. From one perspective, space or time can be viewed as yin (vast, endless, and expanding), from another as yang (bounded, infinitesimal, and contracting). This book will make use of both perspectives—the physical or material viewpoint in the original Spiral of History diagram and the energetic or spiritual perspective in the complementary design. Basic yin yang polarities are listed in Table 1.

Attribute	Yin (Centrifual Force)	Yang (Centripetal Force)
Tendency	Expansion	Contraction
Function	Diffusion	Fusion
	Dispersion	Assimilation
	Separation	Gathering
	Decomposition	Organization
Movement	More inactive, slower	More active, faster
Vibration	Shorter wave, high frequency	Longer wave, lower frequency
Direction	Ascent, vertical	Descent, horizontal
Position	Outward, peripheral	Inward, central
Weight	Lighter	Heavier
Temperature	Colder	Hotter
Light	Darker	Brighter
Humidity	Wetter	Drier
Density	Thinner	Thicker
Size	Larger	Smaller
Shape	Expansive, fragile	Contractive, harder

Table 1. Yin & Yang Attributes

Another way to envision a logarithmic spiral is the popular hockey stick graph (see Figure 8 below). The long, flat handle or shaft represents the long, slow period of early *hominin*, or prehistoric human, development. The comparatively short, upward blade represents the last roughly ten thousand years of human activity. We are situated at the exponential tip of the blade. A third useful metaphor is a rocket ship. The long, slender body constitutes most of the weight, height, and bulk of the vehicle. This is equivalent to billions of years of evolution and several million years of early hominin development. The nose cone, containing the guidance system and the payload, is the comparatively short, dynamic era of Sapiens' prehistory. After reaching escape velocity, human spaceship earth—the five thousand years of the Spiral of History—breaks off and goes into orbit. Viewed as a conical helix, human culture and civilization is the cone, tip, or apex of this spacecraft (see Figure 8).

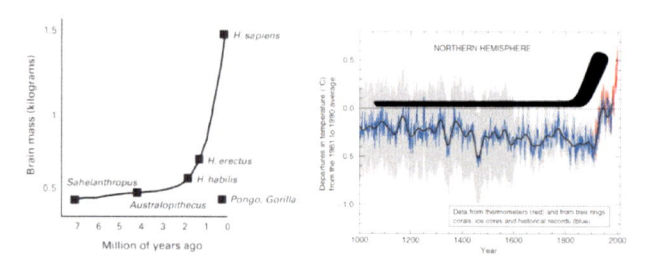

Figure 8. *Left*: Brain mass in the Homo lineage in the last 1.5 million years has increased exponentially, while that of the modern great apes has continued to develop arithmetically. *Middle*: The rise in global temperatures over the last millennium follows a logarithmic pattern. *Right*. The three stages of a rocket ship are another metaphor for the threefold Spiral of History

The Three Eras

We now live at the terminus of a long historical spiral going back eons. Like a nautilus shell (see Figure 9), a logarithmic spiral encompasses three complete coils, each with twelve chambers, for a total of thirty-six discrete segments. In the same way, human development can be viewed as consisting of three millennial eras (though only the first outermost one actually spans a thousand or more years):

> **1. The Agrarian Revolution** spanning ancient and medieval times during which people worked the land, grew most of their own food, lived in settled communities, and engaged in bartering or a feudal economy. As population increased, cities, states, and empires emerged, accompanied by improved transport, enhanced communication, and other material advances on the one hand, and by the advent of monarchy, the priesthood, military, slavery, and subordination of females on the other. The spread of the Black Death and other epidemics posed the first existential threat to modern humans. *The Agrarian Revolution lasted roughly 4800 years*

> **2. The Industrial Revolution** encompassing early modern to contemporary times during which the scientific breeding of animals and crops, the harnessing of steam, oil, gas, electricity, and nuclear energy, and the exploitation of enslaved blacks, indigenous people, and an impoverished urban labor force gave rise to plantations and factories, mass manufacturing, a heavy armaments industry, and a consumer economy that ushered in unparalleled prosperity and comfort for elites and a growing middle class. It also gave rise to a largely secular society, universal education, and a degree of sexual and gender emancipation, as well as competing ideologies, epidemic levels of infectious and chronic disease, and mechanized warfare and genocide. The second planetary threat, the outbreak

of thermonuclear war, receded with the and of the Cold War. *The Industrial Revolution lasted about 400 years*

3. The Digital Revolution commencing with the introduction of computers, robots, cell phones, and other information technologies, as well as fast food, genetic engineering, and other forms of agricultural and medical biotechnology, accelerated life and the pace of change to undreamt levels of material achievement, comfort, and ease. This era gave rise to the Internet, ecommerce, the surveillance state, and a digital economy, as well as GMOs, artificial reproductive technologies, gene sequencing, xenotransplantation (the transfer of cells, tissues, and organs from one species to another), and artificial intelligence. These innovations produced an era of 24/7 connectivity, greater convenience, new forms of leisure, and instant gratification. It also saw the emergence of global warming and unprecedented climate change, loss of biodiversity, the spread of artificial electromagnetic radiation, and an alarming drop in human fertility. These converging trends posed the third great existential threat to our species (and all species), and the outcome remains to be seen. *The Digital Revolution is expected to last about 50 to 60 years*

Figure 9. A nautilus shell has thirty-six chambers

The Sevenfold Spiral

A logarithmic spiral consists of three and a half full turns or seven half orbits. This sevenfold ratio is found throughout nature and the cosmos. Examples include:

- The spiral of universal life includes seven stages of creation: 1) God or Oneness, 2) polarization or the rise of yin and yang tendencies (Qi energy), 3) light, sound, and other waves and vibrations, 4) preatomic particles, 5) elements and compounds (the mineral kingdom), 6) the vegetable queendom, and 7) the animal realm, culminating in human being
- In the physical universe, there is a 7:1 ratio of dark matter (a mysterious, undetected substance that astrophysicists postulate to account for their standard model) to ordinary cosmic matter that shows up on

the detectable electromagnetic energy spectrum
- The ratios of human arms are composed of seven orbits: 1) from the collarbone to the shoulder-blade, 2-4) from the shoulder-blade to the elbow, then the wrist, and the knuckles, and 5-7) from the three joints of the fingers to the tips—all in descending spiral ratios of one half to two-thirds. The tips of the fingers are the center of the spiral. The legs and other bodily organs, systems, and functions follow a similar patter

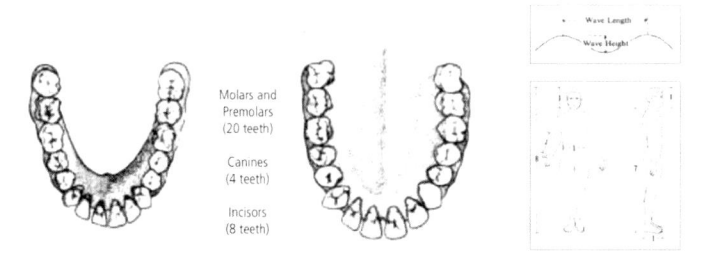

Figure 10. *Left*: The human teeth, with 28 teeth designed to chew and process cereal grains, vegetables, fruits, and other vegetal foods and 4 teeth to cut and tear flesh and bone, suggest that our daily way of eating should be about 7 parts plant quality food to 1 part animal quality food. *Right*: The ratio of the length of a wave to its height (*top*) is 7:1, while the ratio of the head (*bottom*) to the entire body is also 7:1

- The structure of the human teeth forms a 7:1 ratio of 4 canines to cut animal food to 28 molars, premolars, and incisors to chew grain or process vegetables, indicating that hominins evolved eating plant to animal food in a proportion of 7:1 (see Figure 10)
- To balance the 7:1 ratio of heaven's to earth's force, the traditional human diet averaged 1:7 minerals (e.g., salt) to protein, 1:7 protein to carbohydrate, 1:7 carbohydrate to water, 1:7 water to air, and so on to higher waves and vibrations from the infinite universe
- The ratio of beneficial to harmful bacteria and other microbes in the gut averages 7:1 compared to other regions in the body. Known as the microbiome or enteric nervous system (because of neurons in the large intestine), this network largely governs digestive health in the gut and mental and emotional health through the vagus nerve and related pathways
- If properly nourished at all levels (dietary, emotional, spiritual, etc.), human beings naturally develop through seven stages of consciousness, ranging from 1) mechanical awareness or spontaneous, autonomic response; 2) sensory awareness of pleasure and pain, beauty and ugliness, and other pairs of opposite sensations; 3) emotional awareness or consciousness of love and hate, likes and dislikes, joy

and sorrow; 4) intellectual awareness or conscious reasoning involving the general and the specific, cause and effect, and other conceptual categories of thought; 5) social awareness or consciousness of right and wrong, justice and injustice, peace and war, and sustainability and unsustainability; 6) philosophical awareness or consciousness of the quest for the meaning of life, death, and the spiritual world; and 7) universal awareness or all-embracing, unconditional love, endless gratitude, and eternal peace. If improperly nourished, human development typically remains at the second, third, or fourth levels of sensory, emotional, and intellectual awareness

The Seven Ages

The Spiral of History also unfolds in seven orbits and can be viewed as consisting of seven stages, including an introductory or transitional age followed by six ages:

1. **The Prehistoric Age** – from about 15,000 BCE, spanning the end of the ice age, the transition from foraging and sedentism to the rise of villages, towns, and settled farming [roughly 10,000 years or more in duration]
2. **The Ancient Age** – from about 3200 BCE and the rise of agricultural and literate civilization in Mesopotamia, Egypt, ancient Israel, China, India, Mexico, Peru, Greece, and Rome [3500-3600 years]
3. **The Medieval Age** – from about 400 CE and the fall of the Roman Empire in the West and the Han Dynasty in the East to the rise of Christianity, Islam, and feudal kingdoms and principalities [1100-1200 years]
4. **The Modern Age** – from about 1500 and the Renaissance to the rise of the scientific and industrial revolutions [300-400 years]
5. **The Age of Ideology and the Atomic Age** – from about 1900 and the rise of monopoly capitalism, socialism, communism, feminism, and other ideologies to the discovery of the atom, nucleus, and subatomic particles, the development and use of nuclear weapons, and the beginning and end of the Cold War [80-100 years]
6. **The Computer Age** – from the early 1980s and the introduction of personal computers and robots to the development of genetic engineering, biomedicine, cell phones, digital empires, and artificial intelligence [30 years]
7. **The Age of Sustainability** – from the early 2010s and development of competitive solar, wind, and other renewable technologies to the rise of a global climate change coalition and the spread of plant-rich diets in the early to mid twenty-first century [20+ years]

These stages overlap to a degree and encompass many substages and go by various names, for example, the Indus Sarasvati Civilization, Tang Dynasty, Baroque Era, Elizabethan Age, Napoleonic Era, Gilded Age, Meiji Era, Age of Anxiety, etc. Each successive age, or half orbit of the Spiral of History lasts about one third as long as the previous age. The first "hour" or section *Origins*, extending from 3200 BCE until 2500 BCE, spanned about seven hundred years, or the lifespans of twenty people (with an average age of about thirty-five). The average lifespan in modern society today is about eighty, and a person born in 1980 has already lived through seven complete "hours" or sections of the Spiral and can be expected to live at least five more. These twelve sections constitute one complete spirallic orbit of twelve sections, or a third of all the material developments and spiritual advances in human history)! The pace of life today is approximately:

- 5X faster than in the 1980s
- 15X faster than in the 1880s
- 50X faster than in the Renaissance
- 150X faster than at the time of the collapse of the Roman Empire
- 450X faster that when the Spiral of History began with the founding of Sumer, Egypt, China, Mexico, and other complex societies

For good or ill, the scope and power of the economy, science, education, military, and other domains of society have accelerated dramatically during this period.

The Twin Epochs

In describing the ebb and flow of culture and civilization, the flourishing of the arts and sciences, and the energy of food and drink, the terms *yang* and *yin* will be used throughout the text. Representing the complementary, opposite energies of contraction and expansion, light and dark, simplicity and complexity, and other polarities, they find their equivalents in nearly all cultures and languages and partial analogues in modern society, e.g., *philia* (love) and *neikos* (strife) in Greek philosophy, *purusha* (spirit) and *prakriti* (matter) in Hinduism, the *left and right hands of God* in Judeo-Christianity, *centripetal* (moving inward toward a center) and *centrifugal* (moving outward toward the periphery) in Newtonian science, *thesis* and *antithesis* in Hegelian and Marxist-Leninist philosophy, and *superego* and *id* in Freudian psychology.

During the first, or yang, half of each spiral revolution or era, stronger, more dynamic developments predominate, including the birth of cities, dynasties, and empires; territorial conquest and expansion; technological innovations; production of material goods and services; and finally trade and commerce with other regions. Foreign contact leads to exchange of cuisine, languages, literature, the arts, and other social and cultural products. In the illustrations, this trend is represented as the bottom, yang half of each cycle.

The second, or more yin, half of each revolution, or era, is governed by lighter, more idealistic pursuits, culminating in the flourishing of new religions, political systems, and the arts. Over time, however, these can lead to ideological conflict and violence. Following war or peace in the tenth "hour" or section, epidemic disease, famine, environmental destruction, or other catastrophe commonly follows in the twelfth "hour," leading to the decline and fall of a civilization after it reaches its zenith and culminates in the end of an era. This trend spans the top, or yin, half of each cycle in both illustrations. From its ashes, the seed of a new age emerges, and a fresh cycle follows.

The two tendencies, or epochs, that alternate as the driving force behind human culture and civilization for thousands of years can be summarized as:

- **Rule by Power:** a time when material development, advances in metallurgy and technology, trade and commerce, the exercise of state, military, and police authority, and territorial conquest and colonization predominate; a strong, hard, material impulse and wave dominated by masculine energy (the yang, first half of the cycle)

- **Advance by Idea**: a time when values; thought; intellectual, political, religious, and artistic ideals; and control and expansion by ideology and other abstract concepts or by money and other symbolic mediums of exchange prevail; a soft, adaptable impulse and flexible wave manifesting feminine energy (the yin, second half of the cycle)

Keep in mind these tendencies are relative, not absolute. There is still major material development in expansive, idealistic eras and spiritual growth in contracting, technological ones. This complementary opposite unfolding is akin to the black and white dots in the iconic yin/yang symbol. Indeed, some of the most powerful material advances such as atomic energy developed in an expansive yin era, while the spiritual teachings of Buddha, Laozi, and Jesus emerged at the height of a materialistic epoch.

One modern thinker who employed a similar approach was Arnold Toynbee. The British historian introduced a dynamic model of history based on the alternating movements of two complementary opposites, which he termed *challenge* and *response*. In the introduction to his twelve-volume *Study of History* he explains that these concepts originated from a study of yin and yang and that they are indispensable to understanding the movement of human affairs:

> Of the various symbols in which different observers in different societies have expressed the alternation between a static condition and a dynamic activity in the rhythm of the Universe, Yin and Yang are the most apt, because they convey the measure of the rhythm directly and not through some metaphor derived from psychology or mechanics of math-

ematics. We will therefore use these Sinic symbols in this study henceforward.[4]

Glancing at the Spiral of History, Toynbee observes that the prehistoric era, constituting 98% of human existence over the last 300,000 years, was relatively primitive or yin "before entering on the yang-activity of civilization."

The Twelve Sections

Stages of History	Plants	Animals
	Example: Flower	Example: Domesticated Cow
1. Origins	Germination	Impregnation
2. Reform	Sprouts & Roots	Gestation
3. Development	Opening Out	Birth
4. Control	Adaptation, flexibility	Calving
5. Trade	Differentiation	Put out to pasture
6. Humanism	Flowering fruits	Fattening, finishing
7. Idealism	Ripening	Breeding
8. Nationalism	Deepening color	Exhibited at country fair
9. Internationalism	Gathering, harvest	Transported to market
10. War & Peace	Drought, flood, storm	Slaughtered or petting zoo
11. New Dimensions	Casting of new seeds	Different cuts and uses
12. Decline	Death of dormancy	Devoured or natural death

Table 2. The twelves stages derive from the natural order of change

Each revolution of the Spiral of History can be further divided into twelve clocklike sections, vectors, or "hours." These proceed in an orderly sequence and, for convenience, may be numbered from one to twelve. The twelve sections of the Spiral of History are based on natural growth cycles, especially the stages through which cereal grains and other plants unfold (see Table 2). The steps alternate from yang to yin, from more dynamic and active to more receptive and passive phases in the process. The animal life cycle differs but still includes a dozen steps. Note: the plant world is *vertically* oriented toward the world of ideas, energy, vibration, and spirit, while the animal word is *horizontally* inclined toward the physical world governing activity, movement, territoriality, and accumulation of material wealth.

1. **Origins** – A key discovery or invention such as the plow, the alphabet, cast-metal moveable type, artistic perspective, the scientific method, and the personal computer sets the foundation for an entirely new era

2. **Reform** – The adoption of reforms and modification of new technologies enhance society's power and wealth
3. **Development** – The growth and consolidation of empires, kingdoms, and multinational companies through territorial conquest, acquisition, and merger
4. **Control** – Institutions spread and exert near total, or monopoly, control as society grows
5. **Commerce** – Trade and cultural exchange strengthen relations with neighboring and foreign states
6. **Humanism** – New values are introduced that lead to intellectual and artistic cross pollination, mutual respect and toleration, and a highly refined culture
7. **Idealism** – New doctrines and creeds take root and flourish
8. **Nationalism** – Ethnic movements, religions, educational systems, fashion, artistic and musical trends, and sports teams flourish and contribute to social harmony and patriotic fervor
9. **Internationalism** – Faiths, ideologies, and social trends expand and consolidate beyond national borders and spread worldwide
10. **World War or Peace** – Rival ideologies clash and lead to global conflict or unification
11. **New Dimensions** – Following an end to strife, exploration of new geographical spaces or psychic landscapes begins
12. **Decline** – Famine, pestilence, natural disaster, or other catastrophe brings an end to the old social and cultural order from which seeds of a new cycle or renaissance ultimately sprout

As this brief summary shows, the twelve sections alternate between periods of yang dynamism (seed formation and inward consolidation) followed by yin expansion (growth and outward expansion). The three turns of the spiral create distinct thirty-six sections or "hours" in total as they wind toward the center. Overall, the peripheral coil (the Ancient and Medieval World) is loose and yin compared to the inner coil (the Digital World) that is tight and yang. In between, the Industrial or Modern World shares qualities of each. In this way, we can see that we live in a world of multiple spirals within spirals. As relative tendencies, yin and yang are simultaneously present in all phenomena and constantly transforming into one another.

The Center of the Spiral

The Spiral of History unfolds in successive stages, increasing exponentially in speed, compression, and energy in a constant proportion. These are all contracting, or yang, forces, leading to greater physicalization and materialization. The last revolution, or complete turn, of the Spiral from roughly the early 1980s and the introduction of fast food and the personal computer to the mid-2030s will be the time of greatest contraction or yang force in history as we enter and pass through the center. Like a category 5 hurricane, the global energy field we are now entering is characterized by high energy and high pressure, accompanied by swirling gusts of data, surging waves of pixelated images, and battering winds of algorithmic change. Today a toddler with a tablet has more information at her fingertips than the fabled libraries of Alexandria, Baghdad, and Congress combined. Her little brother has more computer power on his game console than the Apollo mission to the moon and more information than is stored in the DNA of each and every cell. More data is created every two years than in all of preceding history. This planetary information storm and supernova of knowledge, the apex of three revolutionary eras now converging, is characterized by:

- **High energy**, including increased use of nuclear power; coal, oil, gas, and other fossil fuels; electrical, microwave, and induction cooking; and cloud computing and increased bandwidth, storage, and streaming
- **High speed**, including faster cars, trains, planes, spaceships, satellites, computers, cell phones, drones, and other machines, devices, and gadgets that will eventually become autonomous and self-replicating. One of the cardinal corporate principles of Amazon, the iconic ecommerce company renowned for its automated warehouses, split-second ease of ordering, and 1-hour delivery in selected markets is "Speed Matters"
- **High temperature**, as the earth warms due to the accelerated pace of change, including increased livestock production and animal-food consumption, advances in transportation and communication, and the overuse of fossil fuels leading to the greater production of CO_2, methane, and other greenhouse gases
- **High density** in bodies, minds, and the atmosphere brought about by the modern way of eating, as well as exposure to heavier molecules released by greenhouse gases that are depleting the soil, lowering water tables, and affecting the vitality of the natural food supply
- **High pressure or stress**, as the pace of life accelerates, ecosystems break down, and many things exceed their natural levels of tolerance and start to disintegrate. This includes the family structure, religious worship, childhood education, governmental institutions, the mental stability of people, and the integrity of cells and tissues, organs and functions, meridians and chakras
- **High production and high consumption**, including increased use of robots, streaming movies and videos, self-driving vehicles, and other networked goods and augmented services, including organ transplants, synthetic body parts, and artificial reproductive technologies
- **High efficiency** as algorithms and artificial intelligence shape and influence all aspects of daily life, including economics, medicine, edu-

cation, sports, legal affairs, entertainment, and other domains
- **High-caloric, high-protein diets**; ultra-processed foods and beverages; energy drinks, probiotics, and other supplements are speeding up the brain, digestive metabolism, hormones and reproductive system, and other body functions and rhythms, contributing to chronic diseases, immune disorders, and new viral epidemics
- **Fast circulation** of people, money, goods and services, transportation, breaking news, emails and texts, neurons and blood flow, and other forms of external and internal movement
- **Short attention span** as time speeds up and space shrinks, leading to short-term rather than long-term thinking; impulsive behavior; a focus on instant gratification, quarterly corporate returns, the bottom line; and personal, collective, species-wide, and spiritual memory loss

As we enter the center of the spiral, boundaries, divisions, and other distinctions start to converge, blur, or break down. Dating is imprecise, and throughout this book time frames are not to be taken as gospel or absolute. The cosmos, nature, and history are governed by broad logarithmic and fractal patterns. But any given phenomenon is a unique constellation of energies that may deviate from the norm. Nothing about the Spiral of History is chiseled or tweeted in stone, and both messianic and doomsday interpretations are avoided in this book.

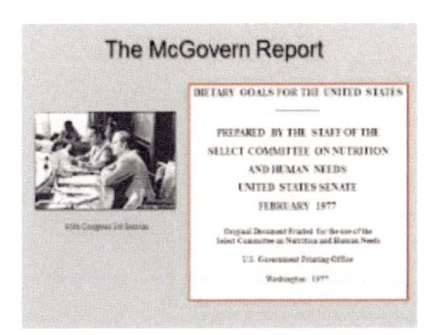

Figure 13. The landmark report *Dietary Goals for the United States* (1977), chaired by Senator George McGovern, led to the Food Guide Pyramid (1992) and the millennial shift from an animal-based to a plant-based diet

As a student of the Golden Mean, I have found that the truth usually lies in the middle between extremes. In the 1960s and 1970s, Michio predicted many of the milestones of our era, including global warming, genetic engineering, and artificial intelligence. He was also occasionally off, e.g., forecasting that cancer, AIDS, and Ebola respectively would spread unhindered and virtually destroy modern society as the Black Death devastated Eurasia at the end of the Middle Ages. On the other hand, the diet and health revolution that Michio pioneered contributed substantially to the planet's first comprehensive dietary goals for these scourges.[5] The U.S. Senate's landmark report *Dietary Goals for the United States* in the 1970s, the Food Guide Pyramid in the 1990s, and the nutritional axis shift from an animal-based to a plant-based diet in the new century directly followed (see Figure 13). By the early 2000s, as society gradually changed its eating habits, it experienced the first decline in heart disease and cancer, and the modern food industry began to be seen as the main driver of global warming and climate change.

It remains to be seen whether Michio's most alarming prediction comes true, namely, that unless we recover our health and reorient our whole way of life, a new hybrid species or artificial intelligence may succeed us as the Spiral of History reaches a climax. He called this process *bionization* and *psychonization*—the fusion of synthetic body parts, digital implants, mind-altering pharmaceuticals, and virtual and augmented realities.[6] New artificial reproductive technologies (ART), including in vitro fertilization and other techniques envisioned by Aldous Huxley in *Brave New World*, his 1932 dystopian novel, are now a reality. They represent one of the greatest scientific breakthroughs in history and have brought the blessings of parenthood to millions of infertile couples. But at the same time, on a species wide level, they pose a grave threat to natural human biological and spiritual evolution. Caesarean Section (CS) has also sky-rocketed in recent years, accounting for nearly half of birthing in some regions. CS is necessary to save the life of mother and child in a fraction of cases, but like male circumcision, it is becoming the default mode for no valid medical reason. Babies who do not experience going through the natural birth canal of their mothers do not receive the rich microbiota that are increasingly recognized as essential for health. ART, CS, and other new artificial birthing technologies are leading unintentionally to what I call Reverse Evolution and the inability of our species to reproduce naturally—the fate of humankind envisioned in Huxley's prophetic novel.

As I write the first draft of these words (autumn 2018), digital implants are being commercialized for the first time. Three Square Market, a small tech company in Wisconsin, offered to implant free microchips the size of a grain of rice into its employees' hands with a capacity for storing ID, medical, and personal credit card records. With a wave of the hand, the workers could pass unhindered through security, as well as purchase goods and services without the need for money or credit cards. Nearly two-thirds of the company's eighty employees volunteered for the implants. While reviewing this section several months later (spring 2019), I heard on the news that in Sweden four thousand people have undergone digital implants. The exponential spread of this trend is breathtaking. Now, just a few months later still (late summer 2019), it was reported that a young millennial software engineer in Dallas had a microchip implanted in her arm that controlled her Tesla. By the time this book comes out, some readers, streamers, or listeners may have paid for it with a flick of their wrist or the firing of a neuron.

The Long, Winding Road

"The destiny of nations depends on the manner in which they are fed."
—Jean Anthelme Brillat-Savarin, early 19th century

The chapters that follow will look at the Spiral of History through many lenses, beginning with the logarithmic spiral itself. After exploring cycles of cosmology, biological evolution, the descent of human beings, and prehistory, we will examine the three complete turns of the historical spiral, beginning with the Agrarian Revolution and proceeding to the Industrial Revolution and concluding with the Digital Revolution. Along the way, we will look at the alternating descending current of Rule by Power and ascending current of Advance by Idea; the seven ages, or half orbits; the twelve hours, or vectors; and the thirty-six days, or individual sections of the unfolding helical calendar. In a study of this scope, it is only possible to highlight some illustrative examples. Profiles of leading personalities on the historical canvas, as well as literary and artistic masterpieces, are sprinkled through the text. In keeping with the spiral theme, the narrative does not always follow a linear order, but rhymes forward and back as new cycles unfold with each cascading wave.

Throughout the study, we will regard diet and food as a lens, or touchstone, for understanding unfolding human destiny. From the *Upanishads* which proclaim "food governs all things, who knows this knows" to the French Revolutionary author Brillat-Savarin who popularized the proverb "You are what you eat," from the Lord's Prayer "Give us this day our daily bread" to the Food Guide Pyramid in our own era, humanity's daily food pattern has been recognized as the foundation for personal health, social well-being, and ecological harmony. We will follow the thread of nourishment—especially the fortunes of grain, salt, and water, the three essentials, but also beans, vegetables from land and sea, fruits, seeds, nuts, animal products, sugar, spice, and other food staples—through the historical labyrinth.

Like a seed, the Spiral of History unfolds as a living, dynamic organism whose communities, societies, and other social units sprout, grow, take root, pollinate, spread, flower, wither, die, and start the process anew. Initial spurts are followed by periods of dormancy, full flourishing precedes decline, and disintegration is followed by rebirth.

The quality of a culture and civilization's daily food largely determines whether its cycles of growth are vibrant and fruitful or stunted and barren. Principal food shapes and influences the health and vitality of society as well as its sickness and decline. It largely governs whether the destiny of the tribe, nation, or era is healthy, just, orderly, and peaceful; sickly, disorderly, unequal, violent, and warlike; or a mixture of both with many gradients and variations.

The traditional paradigm of the successive decline of world ages, in Greek, Roman, and Hindu cosmology, identifies the Golden Age as a long era of peace and prosperity during which humanity consumed wild cereal grains, rarely experienced sickness, and healed with prayer, meditation, and music. In the Silver Age, according to this traditional model, grain-eating declined by about half, accompanied by an increased intake of animal-based food, leading to a corresponding decline in virtue and the emergence of conflict, slavery, and war. In the subsequent Bronze Age, the proportion of plant to animal food continued to decline, and vice, violence, and bloodshed increased to about 75 percent. In the final Iron Age, it was prophesized that whole cereal grains would virtually disappear, and the era would be one of constant strife and bloodshed among families, communities, and nations.[7] The prediction is uncannily accurate, as anyone who lived in the last half century dominated by Supermarket Man and Woman, Southeast Asian and Middle Eastern wars, African genocide, superpower hegemony, environmental destruction, and mass school and community shootings knows all too well. In the Western tradition, the Ages of Humanity are described in Hesiod's *Works and Days* and are depicted in Homer's *Iliad* and *Odyssey*. In the latter, Achilles's Shield—a divine weapon forged by Hephaestus, the god of metallurgy—portrays in meticulous detail the four ages or what the poet calls the "four circles." A modern illustration of the Shield is portrayed on the frontispiece to this volume and is the theme of my previous book *The Circle of the Dance: Achilles's Shield, Odysseus's Oar, Calypso's Axe, and the New Golden Age.*

The early prehistoric era corresponded with elements of the mythological Golden Age, as recent scientific discoveries suggest, including evidence of prosperous, peaceful civilizations in Crete and the Aegean, the Indus Sarvasati Valley, the Niger River Valley, Norte Chico, and Ancestral Australia. Cultivated or wild barley, whole wheat, brown rice, quinoa, and millet formed the foundation of these early historical societies spanning five continents. In each region, there were virtually no violent deaths or war. Peace and harmony reigned for a millennium and a half or more.

Following their collapse, the emerging silver and bronze eras arrived in the form of ancient Sumer, Egypt, Vedic India, Shang Dynasty China, the Inkas, Mayas, Aztecs, and other early civilizations characterized by monarchy, temple worship, the subjugation of females, slavery, human sacrifice, and war. The Trojan War (ca. 1200 BCE), coinciding with the peak of the Bronze and Heroic ages in Greek mythology, was followed quickly by the Iron Age. Domesticated cereal grains, increasingly *awnless*, replaced wild *awned* grains, and proportionately more animal food was consumed. (*Awns* are the long, antennae-like bristles on growing grains that absorb the energy of the cosmos. See the next chapter for a concise discussion of this topic.) The Homeric epics, in particular, extol grain and grain products and warn against their decline and the corresponding increase in violence and war.

Following the scientific impulse of the Renaissance and the Columbian Food Exchange, fibrous whole grains steadily declined as principal food. As animal quality fare changed from festive and condimental use to a regular daily staple, the moral and spiritual fiber of modern society waned. By the peak of this cycle, following World War II and the 1950s, cereal foods remained only in highly refined and processed form in the developed world. Up to 90% of maize, wheat, barley, and other grains were fed to cattle, swine, and poultry to produce factory-farmed beef, pork, and chicken. The widespread intake of white rice, white flour, and degermed maize gave rise to beriberi, pellagra, and other epidemics of malnutrition beginning in the nineteenth and early twentieth centuries.

Figure 14. The Four Ages of traditional Greek, Roman, and Indian mythology unfold in the form of a logarithmic spiral with virtue declining one half to two-thirds during each subsequent age

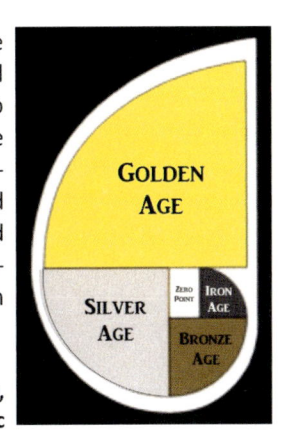

During the zenith of the long Iron Age (known as the Kali Yuga in Sanskrit mythology) and which we may call the Age of Steel, meat, poultry, dairy, and other heavy animal food moved into the center of the diet, marginalizing whole grains, fruits and vegetables, and other fresh foods. In turn, these industrial foods gave rise to "a wave of overnutrition," in the memorable words of the historic U.S. Senate *Dietary Goals for the United States* in 1977, linking six of the ten leading causes of death in society to the modern way of eating. In the realm of public health, the fruits of the industrial era included many wonder drugs, vaccines, and surgical advances that saved and enhanced the lives of millions of people. But at the same time, they lowered natural immunity and made people more susceptible to future ills—a law of diminishing returns seen in such phenomena as the rise of antibiotic-resistant bacteria. For all of its many benefits, the industrial era was built on the African and indigenous slave trade, monopoly capitalism, colonialism, and the exploitation of women, children and racial and ethnic majorities and minorities. It gave rise to communism, scientific racism, eugenics, fascism, sexism, homophobia, ageism, ableism, and other divisive ideologies. Its planetary harvest included World Wars I and II, the Cold War, hot wars in Korea, Vietnam, and elsewhere, and the ever-present threat of nuclear annihilation.

In the last great turn of the Spiral (from 1980 to 2040), the world began branching into two directions as global warming and climate change emerged as an existential threat. The dominant trend—the Digital Revolution—has been a high-tech direction in which daily life is more and more programmed, accessed, and controlled by computers, robots, smartphones, satellites, ecommerce, and other emerging electronic technologies. Fueling this tendency is processed and ultra-processed food, including chemically grown food, fast food, genetically engineered food, irradiated food, vegan meat and dairy analogues, and other debased nutriment. On the plus side, such food is tasty, gives quick energy, and offers instant gratification at an affordable price and with almost zero preparation time. But on the minus side, this way of eating is ultimately unsatisfying, unhealthy, and unsustainable. Besides laying the foundation for chronic physical, emotional, and mental disease, such extreme food breeds extreme solutions. At the social level, these include drone warfare, stealth bombing, cyberhacking and warfare, mass digital surveillance of populations, and geoengineering. The later addresses complex climate change with vast, largely untested, high-tech projects such as weather modification, stratospheric aerosols, ocean iron fertilization, and carbon sequestration.

As Jeffrey Reel, an ecologist and friend of mine notes in his landmark book *Uncommon Sense*, virtually all the proposed solutions for climate change, prejudice and discrimination, violence and war, and the other ills that beset us are pinpoint fixes for the side effects caused by previous technological innovations. In turn, they create a further round of side effects, and on and on in a downward spiral. As Jeffrey further reminds us, there is no waste in nature. Everything is recycled. The billions of tons of pesticides, plastics, medical waste, and other human-made products discarded every year will take years, decades, or centuries to break down. Radioactive nuclear waste can take millions and even billions of years. Nearly all the modern remedies we resort to—from safer, more efficient power plants to faster, more powerful computers—are unsustainable and only compound the problem. In *Walden*, Thoreau put it this way, "There are a thousand hacking at the branches of evil to one who is striking at the root."[8] And that root, as Jeffrey, Laozi, Hildegard of Bingen, and other visionaries through the ages remind us, is healthy soil, nature's greenery and natural abundance—the source of our daily food and of the tree of life, culture, and civilization that springs from its seeds.

Nuclear power, chemical agriculture, genetic engineering, biomedicine, and all the other great scientific advances and breakthroughs of our era are undeniably beneficial in the short run. However, over time, they are unsustainable. The complementary, opposite emerging trend in this third and final wave of the Spiral—the Sustainable Revolution—is organic, holistic, and viable. Beginning with the natural and organic food movement, it has led to a nutritional axis shift in society. As the climate crisis intensifies, it is now widely recognized that the main source of climate disruption—the cattle culture, animal food production, and meat eating—must give way to a plant-rich diet if humanity is to survive. Reduced consumption of animal food has already contributed to improved global health as heart disease, cancer, and other chronic dietary-related diseases have dropped appreciably following the introduction of the U.S. Food Guide Pyramid, British Eatwell Plate, Chinese Food Pagoda, Mexican Food Circle, Saudi Food Palm, and other national and international dietary guidelines. The spread of organic farming and plant-rich cuisine has also coincided with greater empowerment of women, the LBGTQ community, the disabled, the aged, and indigenous people. It has also led to the beginning of gender equality and a measure of racial justice and other human rights advances. On the overly yang side, the modern way of eating, high in saturated fat and cholesterol clogs the arteries, narrows vision, and hardens prejudices and discriminatory behavior. It can sever the natural streaming energy of heaven and earth and block the still small voice of conscience, the universal balancing faculty. On the overly yin side, a food pattern high in refined grains, acid-producing fruits and vegetables, cane and other simple sugars, and alcohol contribute to loss of vision and direction in life, scattered thinking and behavior, and a host of expansive conditions and disorders.

The latest development in the artificial, high-tech branch of the current cycle is the introduction of ultra-processed plant-burgers and cultured meat analogues. The impact of such foods on human health and the environment remains to be seen, but the outlook is alarming. On the one hand, they are moving society in a plant-based direction and raising awareness of diet and climate change. On the other, their high processing and, in some cases, reliance on GMOs, weakens our overall health and vitality and dims consciousness. On the tarmac, revving up for take-off, are *gene-edited foods*. These are foods in which the genome of a single crop is altered but not combined with another species as in the first generation of genetically engineered foods. If history is any guide, these new, improved foods will result in a wave of new immune-deficiency diseases and epidemics and inevitably contaminate the environment. The central existential question for humanity as the Spiral of History climaxes is whether whole cereal grains, other heirloom foods, and new natural strains will remain at the heart of human sustenance.[9]

As the present Spiral of History comes to an end, a new Spiral moving in the opposite direction will be created that will last for another 25,000 years. Coda 1 offers a glimpse of this new Spiral, beginning with a period of transition between about 2040 and 2100, when the North Star Polaris reaches a zenith, a new Precession of the Equinoxes starts, and the slow, gradual millennial-long construction of a new Golden Age begins. The future is quantum and indeterminate, and there are many possible permutations it could take. But I like to think Martin Luther King, Jr. will ultimately be proved right. The arc of the moral and spiritual universe is long and bends toward justice, peace, and love.

Summary of Time Frames

- **Great Year** – the mainstream, scientifically recognized 25,800-year-cycle of the Precession of the Equinoxes, also known as the Platonic Year and the Vega/Polaris Cycle
- **Spiral of History** - the five thousand year cycle of human culture and civilization from roughly 3200 BCE and the advent of writing, the spread of agriculture, and the rise of city-states to the industrial revolution, the exploration of outer space, and the creation of a global,

interconnected world in the twentieth first century. The Spiral of History (including its extended prehistorical antecedents and short transition phase) constitutes about one quarter of the Great Year or Precessional cycle

- **Epoch** – one of 2 alternating tendencies of the Spiral, e.g., the consolidating time of Rule by Power (yang) and the expanding time of Advance by Idea (yin) or roughly the materialist and spiritual halves of the cycle
- **Era** - one of 3 revolutions or complete turns of the Spiral, e.g., the Agrarian Revolution, the Industrial Revolution, the Digital Revolution
- **Age** - one of 7 half orbits, or arcs, of the Spiral, e.g., the Ancient Age, Medieval Age, the Age of Ideology, etc.
- **Hour** – one of 12 repeating vectors of the Spiral that has a unique energy, vibration, or quality, e.g., 1. Origins. 2. Reform. 3. Development, etc.
- **Day** – one of 36 successive sections of the Spiral, e.g., Day 1 The Invention of Writing in the Ancient Age, Day 13 The Invention of Printing in the Renaissance and Modern Age, Day 30 The Invention of Word Processing in the Computer Era
- **New Era of Humanity** – the coming 25,800-year Precession of the Equinoxes that begins about 2100 governed by rising, outward expanding (yin) energy rather than downward, inward contracting (yang) energy.[10] If we meet current social, environmental, and global challenges, the New Era of Humanity could reshape the planet and lead to a harmonious, sustainable planetary, or even solar system wide, civilization that reaches a peak in another six to ten thousand years.

2
THE GOLDEN SPIRAL

"Every time history repeats itself the price goes up."
—American folk saying

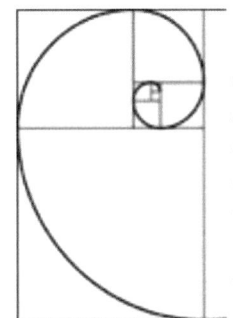

From Ice Age caves to Egyptian murals, from Mesolithic mounds to ancient Mexican pyramids, from Greek pottery to Chinese brocade, from Celtic manuscripts to Renaissance paintings, spirals have been drawn, carved, or woven by generation after generation as manifestations of the universal pattern of change that connects all things.

The universe moves in a spiral. The key to understanding universal order is the logarithmic spiral. This basic form, which appears throughout nature, reveals the mechanism of creation and the fundamental unity and interconnectedness of life. Observing the movement of *yin* and *yang*—the antagonistic and complementary tendencies and force fields that make up all phenomena—through time and space, we discover that their motion appears in the pattern of a *logarithmic spiral* when viewed from the front while their motion is *helical* when viewed from the side. The logarithmic spiral differs from the *Archimedean spiral* (also known as the *arithmetic spiral*) that moves in a linear direction. Named after the third century BCE Greek mathematician Archimedes, the arithmetic spiral moves away from the center or periphery with a constant speed, while the logarithmic spiral has an accelerating speed or pace of change.

The logarithmic proportion governs the structure of galaxies and solar systems, the swirling currents of wind and water, the growth and development of plants and animals, and the contours of the human form. Living according to this fractal measure of natural beauty, harmony, and perfection was traditionally viewed as the goal of a healthy individual, balanced family, and enlightened society. Stonehenge, the Great Pyramid, the Parthenon, the Buddhist stupa of Borobudur in Java, the Great Mosque of Kairouan, the cathedrals of Chartres and Notre Dame, the Taj Mahal, and other monumental structures incorporate this measure (see Figure 15).

44 Spiral of History

Figure 15. Ancient monumental architecture, including the pyramids, the Parthenon, and Taj Mahal, incorporates logarithmic spiral designs and measurements

Artistic masterpieces ranging from Leonardo da Vinci's *Mona Lisa* and *The Last Supper* to the Shakespearean sonnets, Mozart's sonatas, and Beethoven's symphonies also embody spiral principles (see Figure 16).[12] In Leonardo's masterpiece, a logarithmic spiral encompasses her mouth, head, torso, and hands. In Michelangelo's Sistine Chapel mural, the point at which God touches Adam and creates human life is exactly in a golden proportion of 0.618... as the shaded blue and brown lines show. When we visit these places, view these works of art, or listen to sublime music, we enter an energy field that charges and energizes us, elevating feelings of well-being, serenity, and peace. Sound experts recommend marking out a Golden Rectangle in a room, auditorium, or other listening space and placing speakers on the corners to produce the best acoustics. Food prepared or presented in cookware with golden proportions tastes better and gives stronger, more highly charged *Qi* or life energy. In ancient China, millet and other staples were served in ceremonial bronze cooking vessels with spiral measurements.

Figure 16. *Mona Lisa* and Michaelangelo's *The Creation of Adam* are based on the Golden Ratio

Known as the Golden Ratio, the Golden Proportion, the Golden Section, or the Golden Mean, the spiral dynamic is symbolized by the Greek letter Phi. In mathematics, science, and art, two measures (a and b) are in the golden ratio when the sum of the quantities (a + b) divided by the greater quantity (a) equals the ratio of the larger quantity (a) divided by the lesser one (b) (see Figure 17). The value of xPhi is approximately 1.618 . . . and its inverse is 0.618 . . . . The Golden Rectangle illustrates this relationship. A logarithmic spiral consists of a series of unfolding golden squares and rectangles.

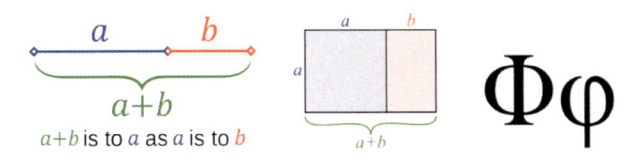

Figure 17. The proportions (*left*) are incorporated into the Golden Rectangle (*center*), symbolized by Phi, the Greek symbol (*right*)

This universal relationship is linked to the Fibonacci series of numbers, named after Leonardo Fibonacci, a medieval mathematician. It begins: 0, 1, 1, 2, 3, 5, 8, 13, 21, 34, 55, etc. Each number is the sum of the two preceding numbers. After the first few numbers, the ratio between every number and its preceding number approaches 1.618. The ratio of each number divided by the one following is about 0.618. (See Figure 18).

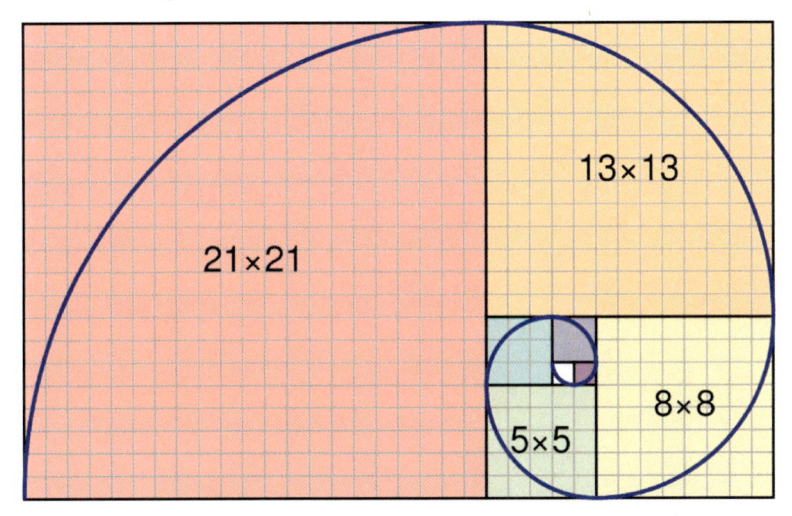

Figure 18. The relation between the Golden Spiral and the Golden Rectangle are illustrated above. The series of unfolding squares has sides of 1, 1, 2, 3, 5, 8, 13, 21, etc.

In astronomy, the Golden Ratio appears in such relationships as the orbital periods of earth and Venus, the relation of the radii of the earth and moon, and the rings of Saturn (see Figure 19).

In nature, the petals of flowers, the leaves of trees, and the components of other plants exhibit the same proportion. The spiral arrangement of leaves on a stem is called *phyllotaxis*. For example, buttercups and roses have 5 petals, pinecones 8 spirals, black-eyed susans 13 petals, daisies 34 petals, and sunflowers 55 and 89 spirals. Such spiral patterns in nature allow maximum exposure to sunlight, rain, and pollinating insects. Similar ratios are found throughout the animal kingdom (see Figures 20). For example, a hawk's wing

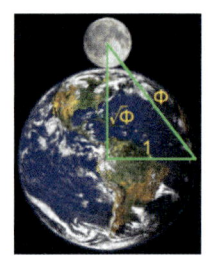

Figure 19. The Golden Ratio is found in the relations among the celestial bodies

has a major junction between its two parts at exactly 62% from its shoulder, and like other birds of prey engages in a spiral pattern of flying that is the most efficient way to hunt on the move. In human beings, the average proportion between a person's height and his or her navel is 1.6. You can measure this yourself very easily with a tape measure or yardstick. The head compared to the upper body is also 1.6, as is the lower body below the navel compared to the area between the navel and reproductive organs. Throughout the body countless logarithmic proportions are found in the branching, tree-like structure of the nervous system, the unfolding of the digestive system, and the circulation of the blood and other bodily fluids. The meridian and chakra systems, which originated respectively in traditional Chinese and Indian philosophy and medicine, consist of streaming channels and swirling nodes of natural electromagnetic energy that radiate through the organism, animating and condensing into physicalized organs, functions, and systems. Each meridian, in turn, subdivides into smaller branches and twigs, bathing each cell with its spiraling energy.

Figure 20. The field daisy has 34 petals following the Fibonacci series. The hawk's wing forms a Golden Section

Spiral relationships are also found in the human form and function (see Figure 21).

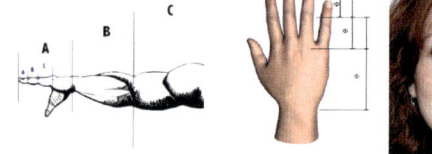

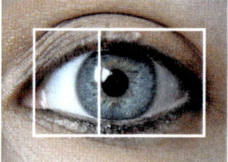

Figure 21. Spiral ratios govern internal and external human structures and functions

The spiral model applies to all phenomena in the natural world. *The Book of Macrobiotics* that I wrote with Michio Kushi (third edition, Square One Publications, 2012) describes in detail the following applications:

• The Spiral of Creation encompasses the evolution of the cosmos from primordial unity or oneness through seven stages of polarity, waves and vibrations, preatomic particles, elements and compounds, and mineral, plant, and animal life (see Figure 22)

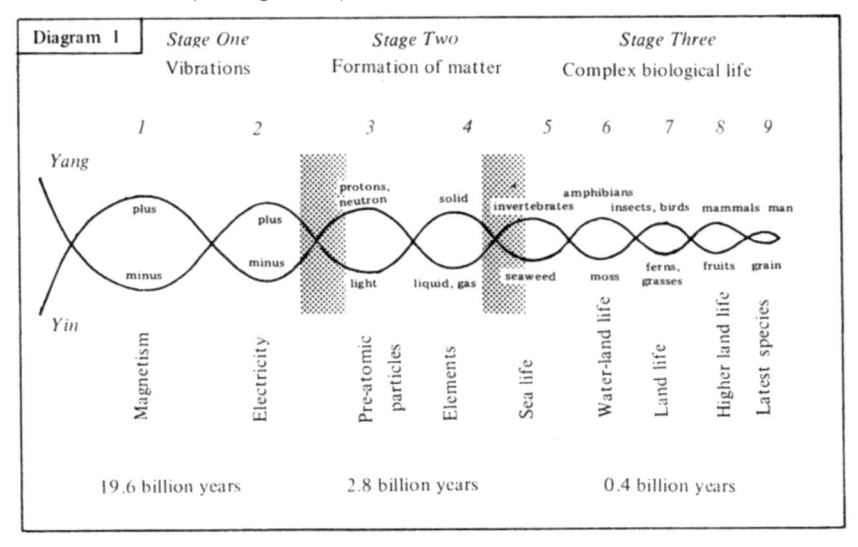

Figure 22. Spiral of Creation: Evolution on earth has culminated in human beings (*top right*) and herbaceous plants and cereal grains (*bottom right*). Note the 7:1 ratio in time at the bottom: 19.6:2.8 and 2.8:0.4 billion years

• The spiral emergence of photons, cosmic background radiation, elementary particles, composite particles, elements, and compounds, including the relative speed of light from superluminal motion to slowed down light that has passed through a superconductor
• The spiral sequence of condensation and diffusion in the formation of nebula, stars, galaxies, clusters, and superclusters
• The centripetal and centrifugal forces that form the earth, cause it to rotate on its axis, and revolve around the sun
• The approximately 220-million-year cycle of the solar system around the center of the galaxy (see Figure 23), creating a Galactic Year with four seasons that governs biological evolution on the earth. Humanity is a product of late Galactic autumn or early winter coinciding with a long period of glaciation, cooler weather, and the mastery of fire for warmth, light, cooking, and tool making
• Biological evolution over the course of 3.8 billion years from the spiral appearance of life in the ancient ocean through the emergence of helical DNA

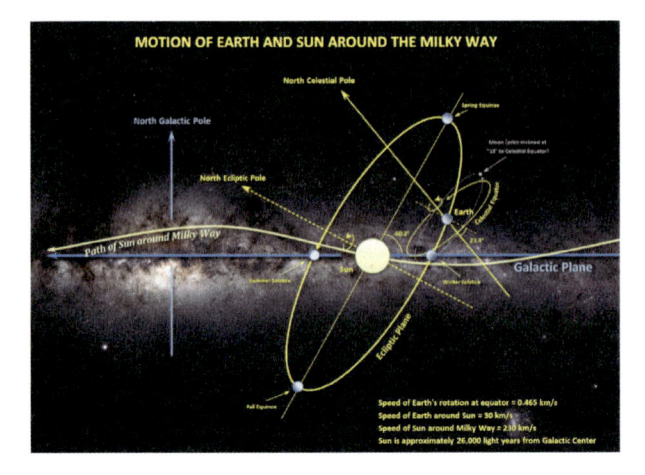

Figure 23. Our Sun spirals around the center of the Milky Way galaxy in a 220-year cycle

in every cell and tissue, single and multicellular life, seaweed and marine life, amphibians, insects, reptiles, early mammals, flowering plants and grasses, primates, and human beings

• The spiral diversity of plant and animal life on earth and the spectrum of more expanded life forms at the equator and more contracted organisms at the poles

• The spiral evolution of the human embryo in seven stages from conception to implantation, fertilization, formation of major systems, organs, and glands in a logarithmic sequence of 7 days, 21 days, 63 days, 189 days, totaling 280 days or 9 months

• The spiral relation between head and body; the digestive, circulatory, and nervous systems; and the spiral intake of minerals, protein, carbohydrates, liquid, air, and natural electromagnetic energy

Scaling Up and Down

In *Scale: The Universal Laws of Growth, Innovation, Sustainability, and the Pace of Life, in Organisms, Cities, Economies, and Companies*, physicist Jeffrey West shows that exponential laws governing the growth of plants and animals and human metabolism also underlie the dynamics of cities, companies, and other complex social structures.[12]

Among the many examples in West's book, the following metabolic rates and socioeconomic factors observe a logarithmic progression:

- Growth rate of plants, animals, and humans
- Heart rate
- Evolutionary rate
- Genome length
- Mitochondrial density

- Gray matter in the brain
- Lifespan
- BMI (body mass index)
- GDP (gross domestic product)
- Safe dosage of prescription drugs per kilogram of body weight
- Length of roads, electrical cables, water pipes, and number of gas stations based on city size
- Distribution of wealth
- Crime rates
- Disease rates

As West points out, phenomena scale at slightly different exponential rates. In the natural world, biology tends to scale *sublinearly* with size with an exponent of about 0.75. For example, an elephant is roughly 10,000 times (four orders of magnitude or 10^4) heavier than a rat (10^1), but its metabolic rate is only 1000 times (three orders of magnitude or 10^3) greater. The ¾ ratio indicates that the heart rate, growth rate, etc. of animals decreases by 25% with increasing size. Hence the heavy elephant is plodding, the scurrying rat is quick.

Unlike organisms, the metrics for cities scale *superlinearly* and average about 1.15. For example, people in a megacity like New York walk 15% faster than in a less populated urban area like Boston or San Francisco. In turn, residents in these coastal metroplexes would walk about 15% faster than people in smaller cities. The scaling rate for companies differs still. For example, the income, profit, assets, and sales for nearly 30,000 publicly traded companies in the United States from 1950 to 2009 follow a logarithmic scale that increases 90% with the size of the workforce. Today, four digital giants—Apple, Google, Amazon, and Facebook—dominate communications, sales, advertising, and many other sectors of the global economy. The force they exert expands exponentially with their size and reach.

The Spiral of History scales at a rate of 0.33 and synthesizes climactic and environmental flux, human activity, the domestication of plants and animals, the growth of cities and companies, and other complex biological, social, and cultural factors. This signifies that each orbit of the seven-stage cycle is about three times longer than the next orbit, or each subsequent stage decreases by 0.67 (which is very close to the Golden Mean of 0.62). For example, the ancient world spans from about 3200 BCE to 400 CE, or 3600 years. This period is about three times longer than the medieval world, which extends for about 1100 to 1200 years from 400 CE to 1500+ CE and the beginning of the Renaissance.[13] And similarly from the Renaissance to the peak of the Industrial Revolution in the nineteenth century to the beginning of the Digital Revolution, history unfolds exponentially.

From an energetic view, the stages and phases of the historical spiral are relative, variable (like tree rings that expand or contract depending on moisture, drought, and other climactic conditions), and dissolve into one another. The end of one era and the beginning of the next form a cusp that includes elements of both. For instance, the Age of Discovery marked the end of the ancient and medieval world and the beginning of the Renaissance. The Space Age climaxed the end of the industrial era and the birth of the new technologically advanced computer age. The key point is to grasp the wave like nature of history and not get hung up on the precise dating of events or on the amplitude, frequency, and other characteristics of the flow. This contrasts with those like Bishop Ussher, the seventeenth century Anglican cleric who dated the beginning of the world to October 23, 4004 B.C. (naturally a Sunday!).

Humanity's Marvelous Origin and Destiny

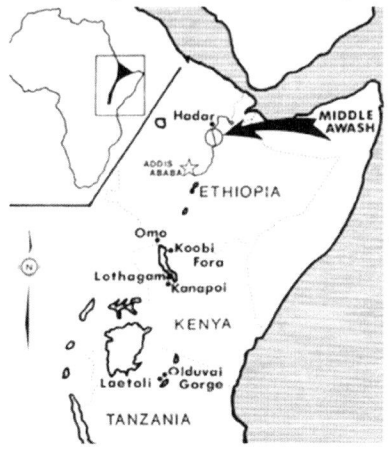

Figure 24. Africa's Rift Valley, Cradle of Humanity

Africa, humanity's ancient homeland, gave rise to a line of ancestral species, culminating in *homo sapiens*. Dinkinesh, whose name in Amharic means "You Are Marvelous," is known in English as Lucy, after *Lucy in the Sky with Diamonds*, a psychedelic song by the Beatles that the archaeologists were listening to at the time of the excavation. The young *Australopithecus* lived 3.2 million years ago in Ethiopia and was bipedal, vegetarian, and tree-dwelling.

The Great Lakes region near where Dinkinesh's skeletal remains were found, includes Nam Lolwe (Lake Victoria), Mwita-Nzigye (Lake Albert), Lake Tanganyika, and other large lakes in the Rift Valley (see Figure 24). Many African cultures trace their ancestry to this area. As E. J. Michael Witzel, a mythologist at Harvard, shows in *The Origins of the World's Mythologies*, there is evidence of an ancient Pan-Gaean mythology (glancing metaphorically at an ancient supercontinent Pangaea) dating to when Sapiens first left the continent in migratory waves. The oldest Pan-Gaean concepts included a heavenly creator, an earthly trickster and culture-bearer, and shamanistic practices involving the generation and taming of heat, communication with animal spirits, and ecstatic trance, dance, and flight to other realms.

According to the most recent archaeological findings of fossils in Israel, our species originally left Africa as early as 310,000 years ago. From there, early humans migrated to the Levant and later the Mediterranean where a diet slightly higher in animal food was appropriate to the climate and environment. The second wave of the exodus went south to South Asia, the

Andaman Islands, Melanesia, and Australia—all warm, tropical regions where a proportionately greater plant-based diet was natural. Successive waves roughly every 20,000 years saw Sapiens migrate in more northerly and easterly directions, including Europe, Central Asia, East Asia, and finally Siberia, where a diet higher in animal food was appropriate in the colder environment and climate.

Beginning with the Out-of-Africa exoduses, human culture split into two broad streams. As Witzel demonstrates, the two tributaries were: 1) the *Gondwanan* (named after a prehistoric southern supercontinent) and 2) a *Lurasian* (ancient northern landmass).[14] The older Gondwana tradition focused on the emergence of life from an eternal cosmos. In some stories, a giant egg or snake gave birth to heaven and earth. Gondwanan mythology was plant-based and saw humans created from a tree or clay. Its culture-bearers included antelopes, gazelles, deer, and more herbivorous animals. From Sub-Saharan Africa where it took root, it migrated to Arabia, South Asia, Papua, New Guinea, Melanesia, Australia, the Amazon, and other hot equatorial climes. A small number of indigenous societies in these regions still follows this mythological tradition.

The later Laurasian belief system focused on the origin and destiny of the world, including generations of deities, semi-divine heroes, humans, and noble lineages. It was animal or hunting oriented and involved internecine war among gods or humans and the slaying of a monster or dragon. Laurasian mythology spread or developed in Asia, Europe, Polynesia, and the Americas and formed the core of ancient Egyptian, Sumerian, Israelite, and other civilizations and cultures in the Fertile Crescent. It also underlay Greek, Roman, Celtic, and other European thought as well as that of the Maya, Aztec, and Inkans. Its sacred animals were the lion, eagle, wild boar, bear, cheetah, and other carnivores. Following domestication, the horse, cow, sheep, and goat—all herbivores—took precedence in the Old World. Today, about 85% of the world's belief systems—another 7:1 ratio—derive from the Lurasian stream, including Hinduism, Buddhism, Confucianism, Judaism, Christianity, and Islam. Socialism, Marxism-Leninism, the modern gospel of progress, and other non-religious offshoots that foresee a secular Promised Land also follow this tendency.

The older, more peaceful plant-rich mythologies flourished over tens of thousands of years. They survived in what I term the Five Peaceful Civilizations that we shall look at in depth later in this book. Though eclipsed by the dominant Lurasian worldview in early historic times, the Gondwanan influence persisted, not only in indigenous southern climes, but also in urban, northern regions. As the Lurasian view spread and gave rise to patriarchal kingdoms and warlike empires, the more peaceful, plant-rich approach was revived by Moses and Isaiah, Buddha and Ashoka, Laozi and Confucius, Jesus and Mary, Socrates and Plato, Muhammad and Rabia, Hildegard of Bingen and Ann Lee, Gandhi and Tagore, Rosa Parks and Martin Luther King, Mikhail

Gorbachev and Nelson Mandela, and other visionaries. The call to reawaken to what my friend Bettina Zumdick elegantly calls, the Golden Dream of Humanity with health, peace, and enough for all is the thread that unifies the human story. It is reflected in humanity's greatest achievements. In the world of literature, this includes the epic of Gilgamesh, Homer's *Iliad* and *Odyssey*, the *Mahabharata*, the *Bible*, Dante's *Divine Comedy*, Wu Chen-En's *Journey to the West*, *Sundiata*, *Parzival* and the Holy Grail cycle, the plays of Marlowe and Shakespeare, the poetry and prose of Percy and Mary Shelley, Pasternak's *Doctor Zhivago* and Toni Morrison's *Beloved*. In the world of music, Gregorian chant, shakuhachi flute, African drums, Indian ragas, Bach's fugues, Mozart's sonatas, Beethoven's symphonies, and many other types of music reflect golden proportions. In the world of art, primitive, classical, Renaissance, and some impressionist, cubist, and other modern art embody spiral principles and themes. And likewise for all the other arts and sciences, crafts and *daos* (disciplines or paths).

Of course, there have been countless unheralded people—mothers, fathers, children; farmers, enslaved plantation and sweatshop factory workers, Black Death and smallpox victims, soldiers and civilians—over the ages who have lived enlightened lives. Over the last five thousand years, the threads of this harmonious, golden heritage have woven a sublime tapestry on the loom of history. The Spiral of History is largely the story of the decline, fall, and rebirth of the unifying principle (the spiral dance of yin and yang, the balance of movement and rest, the marriage of matter and spirit) embodied in these teachings and practices.[15] The Unifying Principle is integral to modern macrobiotics and the teachings of George Ohsawa and Michio Kushi. It is the universal compass of complementarity/antagonism that explains and unifies the world of change, including science, art, history, religion, philosophy, psychology, medicine, and all aspects of life. Practically, it is yin and yang, the universal law of change. The long Spiral of Biological Evolution on this planet (of which the Spiral of History is the culmination) is now climaxing. Whether our species' destiny is bright and peaceful, or dark and violent, or various shades in between, remains to be seen.

The Golden Diet

The Golden Ratio appears throughout nature, history, and all other dimensions of existence and reveals the dynamics of creation and the fundamental unity and interconnectedness of life. The question arises, Is there a human food pattern that reflects this measure and serves as the foundation for health, happiness, and peace?

The dietary patterns of many traditional cultures and civilizations observed the Golden Ratio. For millions of years, our hominoid ancestors consumed awned wild grasses as principal fare and cooked their food over a campfire. Then about ten thousand years ago, cereal grains were domesticated. Millet, glutinous millet, and rice were the main staples in China, Japan, and East Asia. Wheat and barley flourished across North India, the Middle East, North Africa, and Southern Europe. Millet, rice, sorghum, and teff were eaten in various African regions. Oats, rye, and buckwheat predominated in North Europe, Russia, and Siberia. In the Americas, wild rice, millet, maize, and quinoa constituted main food. Except for mountainous regions, deserts, islands, and other specialized environments, whole cereal grains and their products (including bread, baked goods, noodles, pasta, dumplings, and beer) were consumed as a majority of daily food for most of human existence and contributed to our species' unique physical, mental, and spiritual qualities.

By weight, about 50 to 60% of the daily way of eating in temperate climes consisted of whole cereal grains (brown rice, millet, barley, corn, and others), complemented with 25 to 30% vegetables from land and sea, 5-10% soup, 5-10% beans and bean products (tofu, tempeh, humus), and occasional or festive amounts (5-15%) of animal food (including fish, seafood, dairy, poultry, and meat), fruit, seeds and nuts, as well as a small volume of honey, malted grain, or other natural sweeteners, condiments, seasonings, and water, juice, herbal teas, and fermented beverages.

Expressed in ratios among food groups, this traditional plant-rich way of eating mirrors the Golden Ratio of 0.618 (see Figure 24). The proportion of grain and grain products to total food consumed was about 60 to 65% by weight. The amount of vegetables to grain followed a similar ratio. The amount of beans, bean products, seaweed, fish and seafood, and other concentrated protein sources compared to vegetables also averaged about two-thirds. The amount of fruit, seeds and nuts, and natural sweeteners in proportion to the high protein group, follows a similar ratio. The small amount of fermented foods (including miso, dosa, pickles and olives) to fruit, seeds and nuts, and natural sweeteners also approached 60 to 65%. The tiny amount of oil, salt, and other condiments and seasonings also observed this spirallic ratio. Altogether there are seven food groups, and the fractal ratio among them forms a complete seven-orbital logarithmic spiral.

This golden way of eating was reintroduced by Michio and Aveline Kushi on the cusp of the third great turn in the Spiral of History. It served as the biological and spiritual foundation for the renaissance of energetic and spiritual learning that crested with the beatniks, the counterculture, the Beatles, the peace movement, the ecology movement, the psychedelic movement, and other innovative movements in the 1960s, 1970s, and 1980s. The standard macrobiotic dietary approach that the Kushis introduced, based on the culinary traditions of East and West, reflected the Golden Mean in its ratio of whole grains; beans and other concentrated protein products (including about 15%, or one-seventh, fish or other animal food for those who desired it); vegetables from land and sea; fruits, seeds, and nuts; seasonings and condiments.

The term "macrobiotics" was first used by Hippocrates, the father of

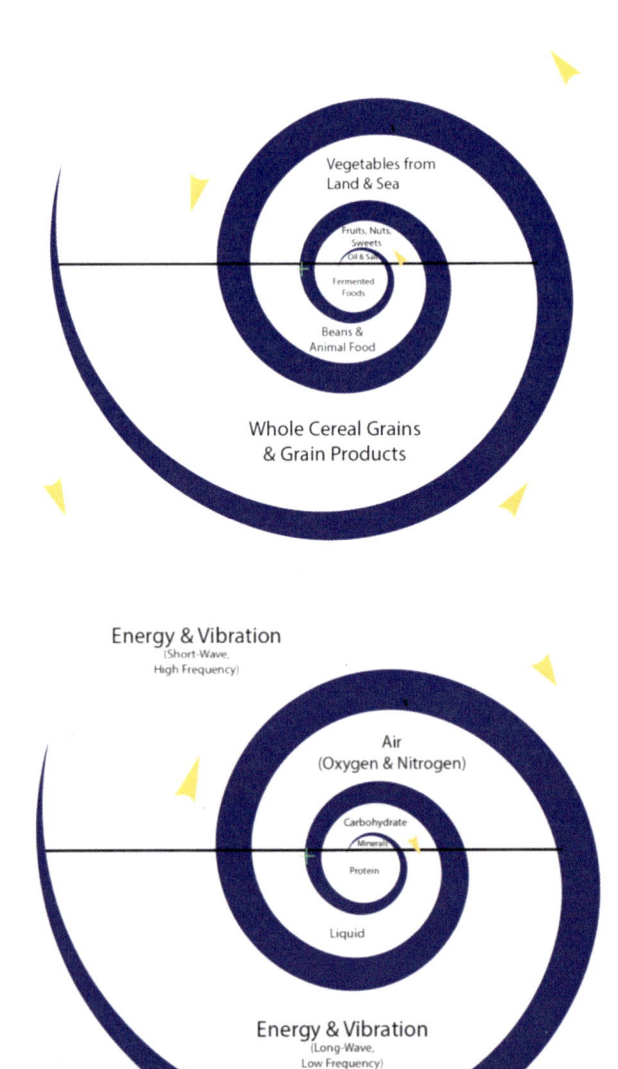

Figure 25. *Above*: The centripetal spiral shows that humanity's traditional plant-rich diet reflects the Golden Ratio. The proportion of grain to vegetables is about 7:1, vegetables to beans and animal food is 7:1, and so on. *Below*: The optimal intake of food and beverages eaten, air breathed, and vibrational energy received follows a centrifugal logarithmic pattern. The ratio of salt and other minerals in the center of the nutrient spiral is about one-seventh of the protein consumed, the protein consumed is one-seventh of the carbohydrate consumed, and so on to the outermost orbits of energy and vibration coming in from the universe. Note: the cosmic waves and vibrations streaming into the planet from the cosmos constitute the greatest amount of life energy we receive and are picked up primarily through awned grains and grain products and through higher consciousness, including visions, dreams, and intuition

medicine who coined the term *makro bios*, meaning "long life" in Greek and who taught "Let food be thy medicine and thy medicine be food."[16] The Kushis did not recommend a single diet for everyone, but a flexible, dynamic approach that differed according to climate and environment, age and sex, level of activity and condition of health, and personal needs. It was plant-rich, averaging about 85% plant food and 15% animal food in temperate regions. This 7:1 ratio is a hallmark of the logarithmic spiral and governs most traditional cuisines in Eurasia, North America, and other four-season climates. In tropical regions, the proportion of plant to animal food increases to 9:1 or more, and in cool and polar zones around 3:2. In practice, the macrobiotic way of eating in the twentieth century has evolved toward an increased proportion of vegetal food because of the accelerated pace and speed of life and rising temperatures, intensified family, work, and other social pressures, and other yang factors. The present-day seafood industry and other animal agriculture are unsustainable, and many macrobiotic friends have adopted a balanced vegan diet. Also, because whole grains are very contracting and on the yang side, their use in natural foods and macrobiotic circles has decreased in recent years to help balance global warming and the accelerated pace of life. These two factors are also very yang—hot and wound up. Since like repels like, people feel more comfortable with refined or cracked grains instead of whole grains and other more relaxing food. Instead of consuming 50 to 60% of their daily food as grains or grain products, the amount has fallen dramatically.

Figure 26. Ancient cookware reflects spiral measurements and enhances the food that is prepared or served: (*from left*) the *jue*, a Chinese bronze goblet for millet wine; a Greek cook pot; a Mexican *molcajete*, a stone mortar for grinding maize; and a Roman stockpot

There are many ways to enhance the energy and power of food besides mastering culinary arts and eating in a balanced way. These include:

- Special planting and harvest ceremonies
- Singing and dancing in the fields to energize the growing plants
- Cooking with love and intentionality
- Preparing food in cookware whose design reflects the Golden Ratio and serving it in dishes, bowls, and cups that reflect the changing seasons (see Figure 26)
- Praying, saying grace, or observing a moment of silence before

and after the meal
- Periodically abstaining from food altogether or giving away your food to others (e.g., once a week or one seventh of the weekly cycle). Note in Hebrew the Sabbath, the day of creation that God rested, connotes seven

By eating whole, natural foods in a spirit of gratitude, prehistoric people were able to maintain their health and well-being, live peacefully and prosperously and acheve their dreams and goals in life. The same principles of balance and harmony can be harnessed today. With beautiful, lovingly prepared food, concord and unity can be created around the dinner table and radiate in an ever-widening arc of love, peace, and universal justice.

3
PREHISTORY

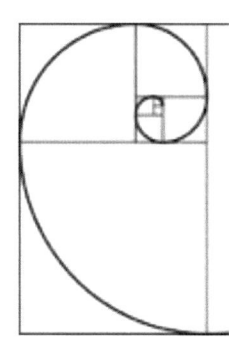

The long prehistoric era of humanity, from its origin through Paleolithic, Mesolithic, and Neolithic times, forms the background to the Spiral of History. This section explores the evolution of hominids, the deep genealogical roots of our species Homo sapiens, and the pivotal role that cooking played in human development. It also briefly touches on the myth of the Golden Age, megalithic technology, and archaeoastronomical sites that point to a highly developed level of energetic and spiritual awareness in archaic times.

The Deep Past

Recent advances in DNA analysis have shed considerable new light on humanity's origin and development. Reductionist claims that specific genes cause intelligence or dullness, heart health or heart disease, and other traits and conditions have given way to more synergistic models of gene interaction, as well as new holistic models that takes into account *epigenesis* or the shaping and influencing of genes by climate, diet, attitude, stress, and other environmental and lifestyle factors. However, new methods of whole genome sequencing are significantly pushing back the analysis of branching archaic human lineages hundreds of thousands of years, as well as making it possible to trace more granularly prehistoric movements and the intermixing of people over the last five thousand years.

In *Who We Are and How We Got Here: Ancient DNA and the New Science of the Human Past*, David Reich, head of a genetics laboratory at Harvard University that has revolutionized the study of human prehistory, shows there were four major population separations (Figures 27): 1) 1.8 million years ago *Homo erectus* went out of Africa and migrated to East Asia. 2) A second split took place between 1.4 and 0.9 million years ago when a common ancestor emerged that contributed to the *Denisovans, Neanderthals*, and *Sapiens*. 3) About 770,000 to 550,000 years ago, the ancestors of Sapiens separated from their Denisovan and Neanderthal cousins. 4) These last two types of archaic humans split from each other about 470,00 to 380,000 years ago. The earliest archeological evidence for Sapiens is in Morocco in North Africa and dates to about 315,000 years ago.[17] The tiny humans of Flores island in Indonesia, dubbed "hobbits," likely descended from Erectus when they arrived 700,000 years ago. Like dwarf elephants and other tiny animals and plants, humans on this isolated island appear to have developed in miniature—a more contracted, or yang, phenomenon characteristic of islands (smaller and saltier or more alkaline) in comparison to continents (larger and more acidic) that in comparison are classified as expanded and yin.

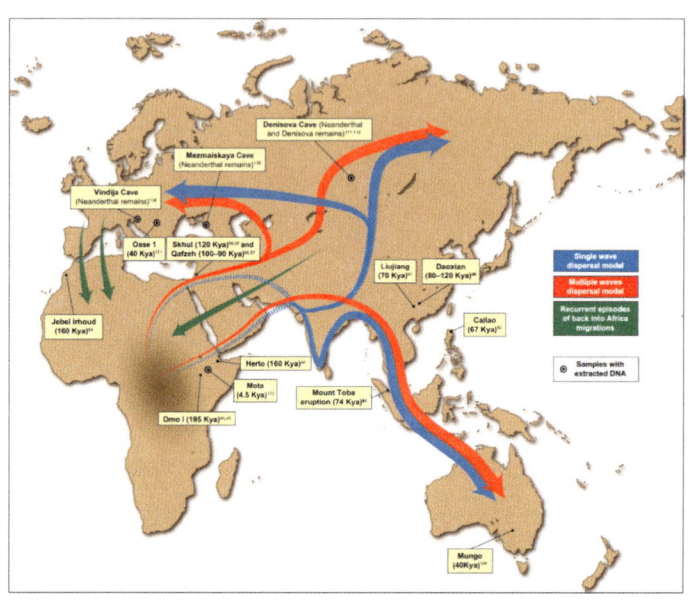

Figure 27. Waves of hominins migrated out of Africa into Asia, Europe, and Australia and in some cases back to Africa in antiquity[18]

The latest twist to this branching is genetic evidence suggesting that the common ancestor of Sapiens, Neanderthals, and Denisovans migrated from East Asia back to Africa. It is also possible that modern Sapiens developed in Asia and returned to Africa. Scientists disagree whether the three branches form a single species or subspecies, but abundant DNA evidence now shows that they interbred—a usual hallmark of a single species.

Between about 220,000 years and 50,000 years ago, Sapiens left Africa in multiple waves, possibly because of megadroughts that pushed them to the coasts. From North Africa, the Northern Route crossed the Red Sea or upper Nile to the Levant, Europe (where a skull dating to 210,000 years ago was recently found), and to southern China (between

Figure 28. Venus of Willendorf, a stone figurine dating to tens of thousands of years ago, was found at a paleolithic site in Austria and may have played a role in fertility rites

120,000 and 80,000 years ago). The Southern Route took migrants across the Red Sea to Arabia and followed the coastline to South Asia, Southeast Asia, and Australia by 65,000 years ago. Among the scores of early human cultures in Europe during the Upper Paleolithic Era, the Gravettian stands out. It spanned parts of West and Central Europe during the coldest part of the Ice Age (about 33,000 to 22,000 years ago) and is noted for its voluptuous Venus figurines (see Figure 28), early musical instruments, and dazzling cave art.

During these exoduses, Sapiens encountered, interbred with, and ultimately displaced Neanderthals and other early lineages that had left Africa much earlier. The earliest contact and interbreeding between Sapiens and Neanderthals took place about 200,000 years ago. Non-African genomes today consist of from 1.5 to 2.1% Neanderthal DNA, with a slightly higher percentage in East Asia and slightly lower in Europe. This is surprising because most Neanderthal skeletal remains have been found in Germany, Spain, and other European regions. Denisovan-Sapiens interbreeding was confined largely to South and Southeast Asia. New Guineans, Australians, and some Indians have Denisovan DNA up to 3-6%. New evidence also shows that several Amazonian populations in South America are related to this southern genealogical lineage (though not west of the Andes in ancestral Inkan regions, Mesoamerica, or North America).

Early Sapiens for whom genetic sequencing provides evidence, but for whom there is no archaeological remains, are known as *ghost populations*. One ghost population, the Basal Europeans, branched about 25,000 years ago into lines of Central Asian, European, and East Asian descent. In West Asia, about ten thousand years ago, people in Israel and Iran had genomes with about 50% Basal Eurasian ancestry. The homeland of this ghost population may have been among the Natufians, a sedentary, pre-farming culture in the Levant (spanning Lebanon and Syria) that tended wild plants, ate gazelles and other wild animals, and constructed large stone structures. Jericho, which they founded, is among the world's oldest cities. Another ghost population that lived about 15,000 years ago—and from whom more than half the world's population today derives 5-40% of its genomes—is the ancient North Eurasians. Part of this group migrated east across Siberia and contributed to about one third of the ancestry of Native Americans (along with two-thirds from East Asia). The other group of ancient North Eurasians migrated west and mingled with Europeans.

Agriculture developed in southeast Turkey, northern Syria, and Israel and spread to Crete and Greece about ten thousand years go and then proceeded west along the Mediterranean coast to Spain. It also moved northwest to Germany along the Danube River, then north to Scandinavia, and west to the British Isles. Cultivation also spread from the Levant into Egypt, Ethiopia, and other parts of East Africa. From Persia, farming expanded to the Indus River Valley in Pakistan and North India and to the steppes north of the Black and Caspian Seas.

The culture that arguably had the greatest impact on modern human development was the Yamnaya. A late Copper and early Bronze Age people on the Pontic-Caspian steppe, the Yamnaya culture flourished between 3300 and 2600 BCE. It is the probable homeland of the Proto-Indo-European language and pastoral ethic that would spread rapidly throughout Europe, the Near East, and India (see Figure 29).

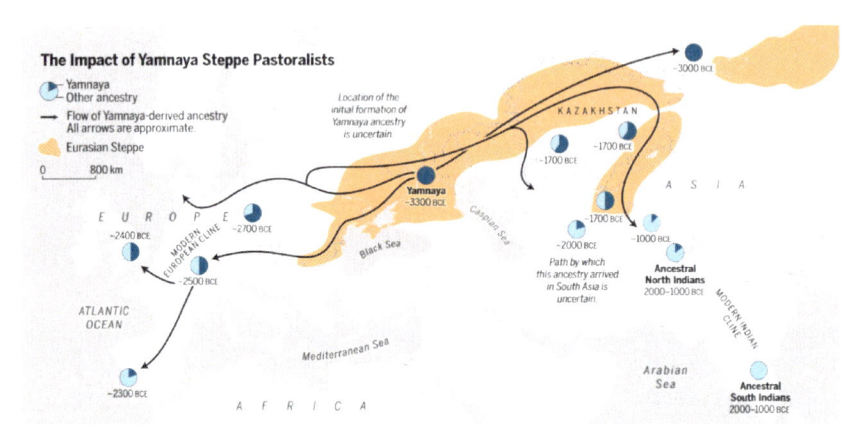

Figure 29. The Yamnaya pastoral steppe culture diffused throughout Eurasia in the third millennia BCE, disseminating hierarchy, patriarchy, the horse, superior military technology, and the proto-Indo-European language, the common ancestor of the most widely spoken language family on the planet

Descended from the Ancient North Eurasians and hunter-gatherers from Ukraine, Russia, Siberia, Iran, and Armenia, the Yamnaya domesticated horses, which made up the main staple in their diet, as well as cattle, sheep, and goats. They also grew small amounts of barley, wheat, and millet near rivers and hill forts but largely adopted a nomadic life. They perfected horseback riding, utilized wheeled carts, and buried their dead in *kurgans*, or tumuli, in a supine position with bent knees and covered in ochre. The Yamnaya, Botai, Shintashta, and other steppe cultures did not systematically invade or conquer neighboring regions, as the early twentieth century theory about the Indo-Aryan advance and the spread of a master race postulated. Twenty first century archaeologists and historians generally believe these pastoral or semi-nomadic peoples diffused relatively peacefully while seeking better pasturage, creating islands of authority, and spreading their revolutionary new technology, lifestyle, and patriarchal steppe ethic along with their DNA through Europe, West Asia, and India.[18] On the Atlantic seaboard, the Yamnaya horizon spread via the Corded Ware, Bell Beaker, and other cultures that flourished in Neolithic Iberia and Britain. Proto-Indo-European languages and culture, especially horses and chariot-driving, also spread to the Iranian plateau, Anatolia, Mesopotamia, and Syria.

The Yamnaya's genetic influence shows up in Star Clusters, or the Y chromosomes of powerful males that produced many descendants. These DNA clusters may originally have arisen from steppe headsmen and chiefs, as well as later Mycenean, Iberian, Iranian, and Indic kings and other elites, who married or took as concubines indigenous females. Hierarchal social structures, patriarchy, and inequality followed this material and technological advance. Their language, proto-Indo-European, developed into Indo-European and evolved into Germanic, Greek, Iranian, Sanskrit, Latin, French, English, and many others. Today, 90% of males in Iberia have Y chromosomes of steppe origin. In North India, the percentage extends up to 80% and in South India about 20%. These new patriarchal societies displaced an ancient matrilineal civilization that extended throughout Eurasia from 6500 to 3500 BCE.

East Asians today are largely the admixture of three clusters: 1) populations based in the Amur River basin in northeast China and Russia, 2) a people that lived on the Tibetan plateau, and 3) Southeast Asians, especially concentrated in Hainan and Taiwan. Ghost populations in the Yellow River Valley and Yangtze River Valley developed millet and rice farming respectively. The Yellow River cohort gave rise to the Han people and spread Sino-Tibetan languages, while the Yangtze River culture gave rise to the great bulk of Southeast Asians and Kra-Dai and other southern tongues. Modern Japanese originated from a mixture of about 80% Korean farmers and 20% Ainu gatherer-hunters. Oceania was the last region to be populated, primarily by migrants from the islands of East Asia.

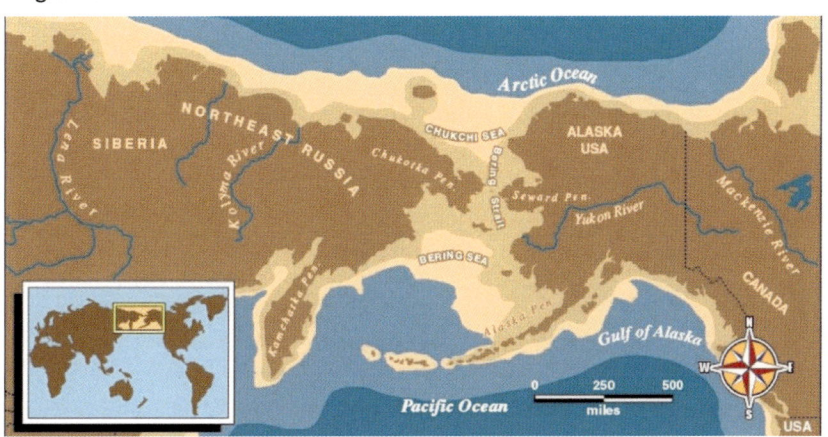

Figure 30. Waves of migrants crossed the land bridge connecting East Asia and North America between 30,000 and 15,000 years ago

Several major waves of migration from East Asia crossed the Bering land bridge and entered the Western Hemisphere between 30,000 and 15,000 years ago (see Figure 30). The astonishing differences among Native Americans, according to geneticists, is due less to immigration from different parts of Eurasia as to physical differences arising naturally since splitting from a common ancestor. Eskimo-Aleut languages, Na Dene, and other North American tongues are all related to Siberian languages that accompanied a recent migration only several thousand years ago. Curiously, the Chukchi, a northeastern Siberian population, harbor about 40% of their genes from Native American ancestors who returned from America to Asia.

A ghost population related to Austroasians, New Guineans, and Andamese gave rise to several groups in the Amazon in Brazil that today harbor from 1-6% of their DNA, indicating that early emigrants arrived in South America across a southern sea route.

Populations that remained in Africa show only about one third as much Neanderthal ancestry as most Eurasians. They also have between 2% and 19% archaic DNA from a common ancestor of Sapiens and other archaic humans. While genetic studies in Africa are less reliable than in other regions because of the deteriorating effects of tropical climate on DNA, emerging evidence suggests that the oldest group of Sapiens in Africa split into four lineages: 1) one passed their DNA to living gatherer-hunters in southern Africa, 2) a second group were ancestors of central African foragers, 3) a third remained in East Africa, from where most of the Out-of-Africa migrations originated, and 4) a long vanished population known as Ghost Modern appears to have lived along the southern edge of the Sahara, remaining isolated from other Africans for tens of thousands of years. Later they intermixed with people from bands to the east and west of their range. About 100,000 years ago, the Ghost Modern split and one branch gave rise to many of today's East African tribes. Another group went west, mixed with Central African foragers, and became the first West Africans.

Between 4000 and 1700 years ago, farming and iron-making technology spread from Bantu-speaking people in West Central Africa to about two-thirds of the continent, spanning most of the east and south (see Figure 31). Many East Africans also share ancestry from cultivators from West Asia (including Iranians), who spread farming and Afroasiatic languages to present day Somalia and Ethiopia about 10,000 years ago. A large ghost population called the East African Foragers contributed ancestry to several divergent lineages, including non-Bantu speaking gatherer-hunters such as the San and Hadza that are among the best-known surviving indigenous cultures today.[19]

In the light of new archaeological, linguistic, and genetic evi-

Figure 31. Bantu speaking people who practiced farming and iron technology migrated to South and East Africa in antiquity

dence, anthropologists and other scientists have abandoned the concept of *race*. Instead, they analyze early human populations in terms of *clines*, or gradual geographical gradients that reflect intermixtures among neighbors. The mean difference between individuals from within any single population, according to Harvard evolutionary biologist R. C. Lewontin and most experts, averages 85%.[20] This translates to about seven times greater diversity within tribes, communities, and other groups than among them. This 7:1 logarithmic ratio, for example, shows up in such traits as skin color and height, which are greatly shaped and influenced by climate, environment, diet, lifestyle, and other conditional factors. As ancient DNA specialist Reich concludes, "We now know that nearly every group living today is the product of repeated populations mixtures that have occurred over thousands and tens of thousands of years. Mixing is in human nature and no one population is—or could be—pure."[21]

Cooking and Human Evolution

Our basic human form and structure is the product of billions of years of biological evolution. From the beginning, the earth was largely covered by water. Sea moss and seaweed evolved in the ancient oceans through the chemical combination of hydrogen and oxygen into various heavier elements, including magnesium, sodium, chlorine, and other minerals. Primitive sea life that ingested moss and seaweed developed into fish and shellfish. Following a series of great earth changes, dry land appeared. Many ocean species died, but some survived and adapted to the new environment. Moss and seaweed evolved into grass and trees, and fish and shellfish transmuted into land animals, eating land plants or more primitive species of animals.

Over time, as a result of further celestial and terrestrial influences, carnivorous birds, reptiles, and mammals became overly contracted from eating strong yang, animal quality food for millions of years and became attracted to their opposite: expansive yin fruits, seeds, and nuts. The new species of primates, including apes and chimpanzees, grew more intelligent and inventive. Over millions of years, their fruitarian diet neutralized or balanced their previous carnivorous way of eating, and they started to experience cold and discomfort in tropical climates in which they previously fared comfortably. Eventually, they sought out a more balanced, yet energizing and warming, type of food. They started to eat wild grasses, the most compact form of fruit that co-evolved in the plant world, along for the first time with root vegetables and other more compact types of plants. Researchers at the University of Colorado Boulder reported the first evidence of this transition in 2013. "High tech tests on tooth enamel by researchers indicate that prior to about 4 million years ago, Africa's hominids were eating essentially chimpanzee style, dining on fruits and some leaves," explains anthropology professor Matt Sponheimer, lead author of the study published in the *Proceedings of the National Academy of Sciences*. "*A new look at the diets of ancient African* hominids shows a 'game change' occurred about 3.5 million years ago when some members added grasses or sedges to their menus."[22] In my view, this is the most important evolutionary study on human origins since Darwin, and I have added italics to highlight the crucial, or "missing link" between grasses (that include wild cereal grains) and the evolution of human beings.[23]

Although grasses (wild grains) and sedges (a family of rushes including water chestnut) were widely available before then, primates ignored them for a long period. "We don't know exactly what happened," observes Sponheimer. "But we do know that after about 3.5 million years ago some of these hominids started to eat things that they did not eat before, and it is quite possible that these changes in diet were an important step in becoming human."[24]

This early African primate species, the ancestor of human beings, consumed the wild grasses and other plants raw. But in the course of another million or more years, their intellect developed, they stood upright, and they discovered how to use fire for cooking. The end result was early human ancestral lines, including Habilis, Erectus, Neanderthalensis, Denisovan, and eventually Sapiens (see Figure 32).

Mastery of cooking led to a revolution in all aspects of life as well as food preparation and eating. Chimpanzees, apes, and other primates spend most of the day chewing on raw seeds, nuts, and fruits. The discovery of fire and advent of cooking about 1.5 to 2 million years ago in East and South Africa led to the emergence of hominins that were physically, mentally, and spiritually more advanced than other primates. "The absence of a ridge on the top of the skull, where muscles that power chewing and biting would be attached, shows that the jaw was smaller than it was when individuals needed strength to chew lots of tough [raw] plant material," notes Mary Soderstrom in *Road Through Time*, commenting on skeletal remains dating to about 800,000 years ago. "This lack of strong muscles strongly suggests, in fact, that the individual had begun to cook food on a regular basis."[25]

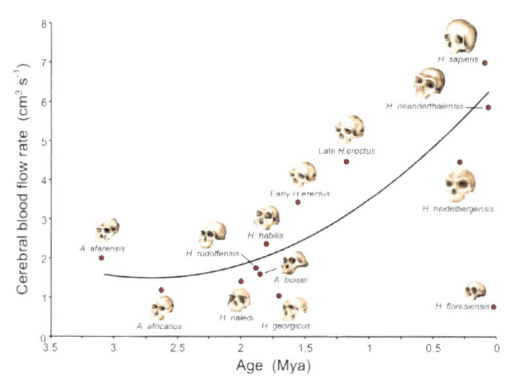

Figure 32. Human mental and cognitive abilities increased expoentially from Australopithecines to Sapiens as early humanity mastered fire and cooking[26]

Cooking also brought other physiological and social changes, including a more highly developed brain and cognitive abilities, shorter intestines, and more versatile hands and thumbs. Evolving humans needed only 2 to 3 hours a day to prepare and cook their food instead of 6 to 9 hours or more in the case of monkeys, chimpanzees, and apes (a roughly 1 to 3 ratio) eating exclusively raw food. Along with enjoying greater free time from less chewing, these structural changes gradually enabled them to make tools, develop art, language, and culture, and create new forms of community and social organization. Cooking is not exclusively human, and there are many animals, including bonobos and chimpanzees that use tools to obtain, process, or warm up their food (see Coda 3: Proto Cooking by Mammals, Birds, and Insects). But humans were the only species that systematically cooked their food and transformed it into the central art of their culture.

For nearly 2 million years, the primary hominin ancestor in Africa, *Australopithecus* was largely vegetarian. For example, *Australopithecus anamensis*, a hominin that lived in East Africa more than 4 million years ago, was herbivorous. According to a recent study at the University of Barcelona, its diet consisted of wild grasses, seeds, sedges, tubers, and fruits and was similar to that of other primates, including baboons and the green monkey, that live in shrubby savannah marked by seasonal changes.[27]

Dinkinesh lived about a million years later. Her skeletal remains, found in East Africa, classify her as *Australopithecus afarensis*. Also known as Lucy, Dinkinesh was vegetarian, eating grasses and leaves, as well as fruit, nuts, seeds, and tubers. A contemporary upright hominin known as *Paranthropus boisei* was initially dubbed Nutcracker Man because of its large, flat teeth and powerful jaws. However, in the light of new findings, scientists now believe Nutcracker Man used its back teeth to grind grasses and sedges. Compared to monkeys, early human brains and central nervous system are more compact, or yang, from eating cereals. The human spinal cord is contracted, whereas the monkey has a tail that is a lengthening, or an extension, of the nervous cord and may be classified as more yin.

With the evolution of Habilis and Erectus, about 2.5 to 1.8 million years ago, brain size increased dramatically. Stone tool making, language, and other cultural breakthroughs accompanied the rise of these new hominin lineages. Anthropologists attribute these innovations to a prolonged cooling and drying trend that spread across Africa at this time, transforming forests into grasslands. This was the probable result of a partial axis shift that brought cooler weather and the emergence of savannahs. Increased climate variation contributed to greater dietary flexibility and the development of hunting, scavenging, and fishing. The introduction of high-caloric, high-density meat, fish, and seafood into the hominin diet during this glacial era contributed to smaller stomachs and colons, making more energy available for neurological development. Additional calories from wild game and fish may have also allowed women to have shorter intervals between pregnancies and to give birth to more children, spurring population growth. Menarche, or first menstruation, typically begins at a much earlier age in pubescent girls in today's modern urban society (13 years old) than in the nineteenth century (15 years old). Over the last twenty years, the age has dropped to as young as ten.[28] Increased animal food consumption appears to be the main factor.

For the most part, the early human diet was plant-based. As forensic evidence suggests, wild game was passively scavenged rather than actively hunted for many hundreds of thousands of years and represented a small, opportunistic consumption of animal food.[29] Only much later, in response to advancing glacial ice and other climatic changes, did big-game hunting come into season. Contemporary hunter-gatherer societies such as the San and Kalahari bushmen in Africa today continue to consume the vast majority of their food in the form of foraged plants, fruits, and nuts and only small amounts, between 10-20%, in the form of animal food.[30]

Figure 33. The San of South Africa use traditional technology to make fire and cook

In *Catching Fire: How Cooking Made Us Human,* Harvard primatologist and professor of biological anthropology Richard Wrangham concludes that the mastery of fire for cooking spurred the development of early humans (see Figure 33). Cooking, in his view, made more calories from existing, largely plant quality food available and improved metabolism, leading to the development of larger brains. Cooking also facilitated warmth, leading to the loss of body hair and the ability to run faster without overheating. Wrangham suggests it also allowed early hominins to develop more peaceful personalities, fashion new social structures around the hearth, and bring the sexes closer together. Over time, raw food, he contends, does not supply enough caloric energy and is unsustainable and can cause women to cease menstruation. Cooking increases the net energy gain by 30%.[31] As humans evolved from the monkey and primate state, they adapted to changing climates and environments, harmonized with seasonal change, found new ways to gather and store food, and mastered fire.

Fire is very yangizing—activating, warming, and intellectually and technologically stimulating. It may have led early hominins to leave Africa for the first time about 2 million years ago. Erectus migrated throughout Eurasia and settled as far away as present-day Georgia (bordering Russia not Florida), India, China, and Indonesia. Fire allowed them to live and flourish in colder regions and develop more refined tools.

In his most recent research, Wrangham has studied the comparative influence of chimpanzees and bonobos on human evolution. Since Darwin's time, it was thought that humans descended from the great apes, especially chimpanzees that exhibit a high degree of violent behavior in the wild. This aggressiveness by our closest evolutionary cousin was cited as a model for human development and appeared to provide a biological explanation for humanity's long history of interpersonal violence, domination of females, and war. In recent years, it has been discovered that humans are actually more closely related to bonobos, a lesser known variety of ape that shares a common ancestor with chimpanzees. In the wild, bonobos are extremely peaceful, avoiding violence in the troop and with outsiders, preferring to resolve disputes by initiating sexual relations.

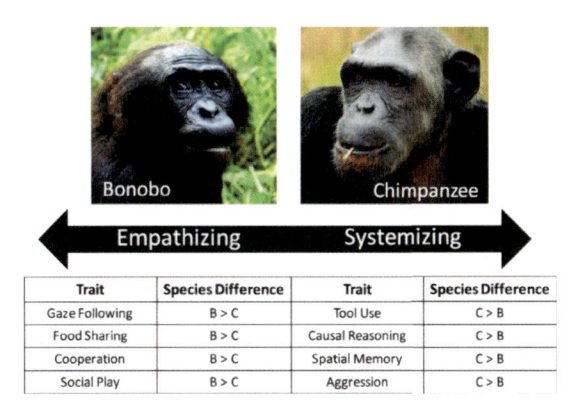

Trait	Species Difference	Trait	Species Difference
Gaze Following	B > C	Tool Use	C > B
Food Sharing	B > C	Causal Reasoning	C > B
Cooperation	B > C	Spatial Memory	C > B
Social Play	B > C	Aggression	C > B

Figure 34. Cognitive and behavioral differences between chimpanzees (C) and bonobos (B)[32]

Frans de Waal, a Dutch primatologist, describes bonobo society as altruistic, compassionate, empathetic, kind, patient, and sensitive. It is also matriarchal with females of the species taking the lead. In contrast, chimpanzees are patriarchal, males dominate females, and troupes send out all-male hunting expeditions to seek meat. They are highly territorial and will kill other males. Based on gene sequencing, researchers at Max Planck Institute reported in 2005 that humans share slightly more DNA with bonobos than chimpanzees. Subsequent studies have found that humans share 1.6 percent of their DNA only with bonobos, not chimpanzees. This translates into closer musculature, brain size, metabolism, and social behavior. Bonobos are omnivores, eating primarily fruit, leaves, bark, stems, roots, and other plant foods, as well as a small amount of insect larvae, worms, crustaceans, honey, and eggs. They eat tiny amounts of meat, including flying squirrels or duikers (small antelopes). Chimpanzees consume more meat, including infants of other females, but do not eat the bodies of slain adults from other groups.

This fascinating, newly discovered primate heritage suggests that genetically early humans synthesized elements of both bonobos and chimpanzees. Compared to each other, bonobos are more yin, or relatively kind, gentle, and harmonious, while chimpanzees are more yang, or active, systematizing, and aggressive (see Figure 34). Clearly, humanity's long history combines elements of both lineages. But as the latest scientific studies are showing, the arc of biological evolution bends toward gentleness, cooperation, peace and harmony. Table 3 summarizes the diet and behavior of early hominids lineages.

Harvesting Wild Grains

Archaeological evidence confirms that Sapiens have been harvesting, processing, and consuming wild cereal grains for much of its existence. Stone tools found in East Africa, the cradle of humanity, indicates that people were processing sorghum 100,000 years ago. In Ngalue, a cave in Mozambique, researchers discovered an assortment of seventy stone tools in a layer of sediment deposited on the cave floor 42,000 to 105,000 years ago. Although the tools cannot be dated precisely, those in the deepest strata appear to be at least 100,000 years old. About 80% of the tools, including the scrapers, grinders, points, flakes, and drills, had ample starchy residue, archaeologists told *Science*.[33] Eighty-nine percent of the starches came from sorghum, a whole cereal grain that still constitutes a main staple in many parts of

Species	Era	Region	Principal Food	Supplemental Food	Activities
Organutan	Split from ape line in Africa 16-19 million years ago	Malaysia and Indonesia	Fruit (60%), mineral-rich soil, bark, leaves, shoots	Insects, eggs, and small vertebrates	Forages one third of the day
Gorilla	Diverged from a common ancestor 7 millions years ago	Central Africa	Leaves (85%), vines, wild celery, roots, flowers, fruit, grubs	Termites	Eats 40 lb. of plants daily and sleeps 18 hours
Chimpanzees and Bonobos	Diversed 7 million years ago	Central Africa	Fruit, tree seeds, flowers, soft pith, resin, bark	2% termites, flying squirrels, and antelopes; chimps eat more meat	Chimps patriarchal, aggressive; Bonobos matriarchal, peaceful
Austrolopithicus afarensis	3-4 million years ago, includes Lucy, earliest hominin	East Africa	Wild uncooked grasses, fruit, sedges, nuts, seeds	Small volume of raw animal food	Thick jaws, large molars, walks upright, small brain
Australopithicus robustus	1.2 - 2 million years ago	East Africa	Wild grasses, hard, gritty food, nuts, tubers	Small amount of animal food	Large jaws, small brain
Homo Habilis	1.4 - 2.3 million years ago	East Africa	Wild grasses, sedges, fruit, wild plants	Small volume insects and other raw animal food	First stone tools, speech

Homo Erectus	1 - 1.8 million years ago	Africa, China, India, Java, Caucasus	Wild grasses (cooked) seeds, fruits, nuts, and other plants	Wild game, hunted, scavenged, and cooked (5-10%)	Discovery of fire and cooking; reduced gut size and large brain (75% modern size)
Homo neanderthalensis	130,000 to 350,000 years ago, went extinct in Europe 24,000 years ago	Europe, Western Asia, Siberia and East Asia	Wild grasses, tubers, sees, nuts (raw and cooked)	Larger volume of meat (up to 50%), though at least one community was vegan	Developed in cold, glacial era; large cranium; earliest burials; tools; cooking; healing plants; interbred w/sapiens
Homo denisovan	Diverged from common lineage with Neanderthals and Sapiens about 750,000 years ago	Siberia, Southeast Asia, Australia	Wild grasses, tubers, berries, nuts (raw and cooked)	Probably similar to Neanderthals	Robus species; made a bracelet found in a Siberian cave; interbred with Neanderthals and Sapiens
Homo floresiensis	12,000 to 100,000 years ago and possibly 800,000 years ago	Indonesia	Foraging plants	Dwarf elephants and other animal food	Dwarf "Hobbit" species; used stone tools and ate cooked food
Homo sapiens (modern humans)	315,000 years or more to the present	East Africa, Morocco, Israel, Greece, and eventally worldwide	Wild awned and cultivated grains; bread; veggies, tubers, fruit, nuts, seeds, sea veggies, fermented food	Meat, poultry, fish seafood, primarily-cooked (about 5-20%), more in cold, mountainous desert climates	Cereal grain processing dates to 100,000 years ago; then farming, cities, industry, and digitalization

Table 3. Diet and Behavior of Early Hominids

parts of Africa. The rest came from the African wine palm, the false banana, pigeon peas, wild oranges, and the African potato. The evidence suggests that people living in Ngalue brought starchy plants, especially sorghum, to their dwelling where it was made into porridge and baked in the form of flat bread and other products.

In multiple European sites, including present-day Moravia, Italy, and Russia, evidence has also surfaced of ancient grain harvesting, cooking, and processing dating to about 25,000 to 30,000 years ago during a Stone Age era renowned for its spectacular Ice Age cave paintings and elegant Venus figurines. For example, mammoth hunters in Dolni Vestonice, an Upper Paleolithic site in Moravia, had sickle blades and grinding stones. They harvested edible seeds of wild grasses, the common reed, bog bean, water nut, and arctic berries. Remains of plant food preserved by a hearth at Dolni Vestonice II dating to from 27,000 to 24,000 years ago contained a seed, tissues from roots and tubers, possible acorn mush, and wood charcoal. In the Black Sea region, archaeologists unearthed thousands of small blades made of flint and hafted with bitumen into bone handles to harvest wild grasses and cane. As Dr. Revedin of the Italian Institute of Prehistory and Early History in Florence concluded: "The discovery of grain and plant residues on grinding stones at the three sites suggests plant-based food processing, and possibly flour production, was common and widespread across Europe at least 30,000 years ago."[34]

In North America, Clovis hunters used seed-grinding stones at Medicine Lodge Creek, Lookingbill, and sites in the High Plains dating to about 12,000 years ago. Ancient storage pits yielded remains of food seeds from pine, juniper, cactus, prune, sunflower, and amaranth.[35] Paleolithic sites around the world have pits dug into the earth that appear to have been used for food storage, including wild grains and nuts. Australian aborigines relied on wild strains of indigenous rice, millet, roots, tubers, fruit, and seeds for their daily fare. In Papua New Guinea, starch from wild sago palms served as a main energy source.

Cooking and food quality may have also shaped and influenced human speech. According to a recent study, farming resulted in the consumption of more softly cooked plant foods that modified the human bite and enabled early cultivators to pronounce certain sounds that animal-food eating hunters couldn't make. "Certain sounds like these 'f' sounds are recent, and we can say with fairly good confidence that 20,000 or 100,000 years ago, these sounds just simply didn't exist," says researcher Balthasar Bicklet, a University of Zurich linguist.[36] Based in part on observing contemporary hunter-gatherers, the theory holds that softly cooked plant foods transformed the teeth and jaw, producing an overbite that was able to make the 'f,' 'v,' and other labiodental sounds. What the original prehistoric F-word was remains unknown, but it didn't begin with F.

The Spiral of Human Evolution

This long process of early human evolution can be viewed as a logarithmic spiral with three complete revolutions:

1. The Discovery of Principal Food - The consumption of raw wild grasses (including sorghum, millet, rice, and other wild grains) distinguished *Homo* from earlier primate lines that ate primarily fruits, seeds, and nuts [about 3 to 4 million years ago]

2. The Discovery of Fire and Cooking - The mastery of fire led to the development of cooking and the probable introduction of language, storytelling, and myth around the campfire [about 1½ to 2 million years ago]

3. The Development of Tools - The earliest tools made of stone, rock, bone, shell, and other more durable substances, as well as wood, fibers, vines, bark, and other more perishable items, were used for gathering, hunting, food preparation, shelter, and clothing [about 1 million to 500,000 years ago]

Similar to the Spiral of History with its three stages of development (Agricultural, Industrial, and Digital), the preceding era, or what we may call the Spiral of Human Culture, has three revolutions. Each complete turn lasted about three times longer than the following turn. As in the historical spiral, each of the three prehistorical revolutions can be divided into epochs of 1) yang material development and 2) yin artistic or intellectual advance. Including the initial, transitory stage, humanity's cultural journey can be seen as spanning seven orbital ages or half turns:

1. **The Age of Transition from Primate to Human** – A time of major climactic change, including cooler temperatures, that turned large parts of Central and Southern Africa from forest and jungles into savannah and grassland [roughly 12 to 6 million years ago]
2. **The Age of Wild Grasses and Cereal Grains** – The introduction of raw wild grasses, such as the ancestors of sorghum, millet, and rice, into the hominin diet, and the earliest stone tools [about 4 million years ago]
3. **The Age of Sedges and Wild Vegetables** – The use of proportionately more plant food, including sedges, roots, and tubers, in the hominin diet [about 4 – 3 million years ago]
4. **The Age of the Discovery of Fire** – The mastery of fire for use in providing light, warmth, and protection from predators [about 2 – 1.5 million years ago]
5. **The Age of Cooking and Language** – Human speech probably dates back to Habilis and Erectus and the use of fire for cooking and use of tools [about 1.8 to 1.5 million years ago]. Cooked grains in particular appear to have strengthened (yangized) the *hyoid* (the small, irregular bone in the throat that descends in conjunction with the larynx) that makes speech possible and may have led to storytelling around the campfire
6. **The Age of Cloth, Shells, and Metals** – The introduction of fabrics made from leaves, grass, vines, fur, and leather; the use of shells for beads and jewelry; and the use of gold and silver, as

well as copper, tin, and meteorological iron for tools, adornments, and weapons goes back to Middle Paleolithic times [about 500,000 to 50,000 years ago]
7. **The Age of Art and Ritual** – The arts of music, dance, and pictorial art, as well as ritual cremations and burials, date to the upper Paleolithic era [about 100,000 – 20,000 years ago] (see Figure 35)

Figure 35. The world's oldest musical instruments are flutes made of bird bone and mammoth ivory from southern Germany and dating to 40,000 years ago

This large Spiral of Human Culture, spanning several million years, served as the foundation for the Spiral of History.

The Golden Age

"There have been, and will be again, many destructions of mankind arising out of many causes; the greatest have been brought about by the agencies of fire and water."
—Plato, Timaeus

Human destiny is strongly influenced by the cycle of northern celestial motion, the approximately 25,800-year cycle of the Precession of the Equinoxes. The Precession was first described in writing by the Greek philosopher Hipparchus in 127 BCE and confirmed over the centuries by many observers and astronomers. Early Western thinkers referred to it as the Platonic Year. In astrology, the roughly 26,000-year cycle was divided into twelve houses and gave rise to the Ages of Ares, Pisces, Aquarius, etc. In that cycle—depending on how the earth's axis is aligned relative to the plane of our galaxy—we receive varying amounts of stellar and solar radiation, electromagnetic energy, and other impulses and waves originating from the center of the Milky Way as well as the billions of other galaxies in the infinite universe that imprint unique qualities that shape and influence our character and destiny.

As the sun and planets journey around the galactic center, their orbit traces a gentle wavelike motion. From a point removed from the earth, our planet would be seen to wobble slowly like a child's top, with its north-south axis pointing first in one direction, then in the other, making one complete wobble about every 26,000 years. That wobbling motion of the earth's axis traces a circle in the night sky, with a series of stars in the northern constellations serving successively as Pole Star (see Figure 36). In the lifetime of any individual or society, the movement is imperceptible—only 1 degree every 72 years. But over millennia, there is a slow, steady, perceptible celestial shift.

As a whole, the earth is surrounded by a vast protective belt of electromagnetic fields, but the area over the poles is relatively open. The shower of energy from the heavens exerts a stronger influence in these regions than at the equator; as a new star or constellation moves into ascendancy it produces a regular change of electromagnetic charge on the earth. In comparison to the South Pole that is facing more toward the center of the galaxy, the North Pole is angled toward the periphery, receiving energy from billions of other galaxies. As a result, the North is more highly charged than the South.

The Great Year falls into two halves, each lasting about 13,000 years, which have been traditionally described as the Age of Light and the Age of Darkness, the Time of Paradise and the Time of Wilderness, Spiritual Civilization and Material Civilization, or other complementary opposites. The Precessional cycle can further be divided into four seasons: first, *summer* and the peak of light; next *fall* and the waning of light; then, *winter* and the depth of darkness; and finally, *spring* and the return of the light. Transitional stages of four more constellations between these four points make a total of eight constellations in the Great Year.

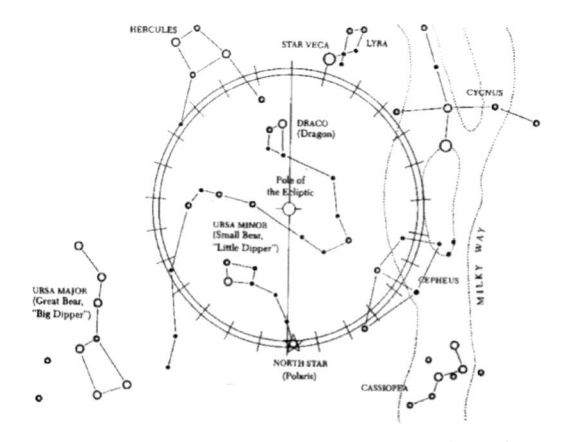

Figure 36. The Precession of the Equinoxes causes bright stars in several different constellations to appear overhead and serve as the new North Star about every three thousand years

About twenty to twenty-five thousand years ago, during Precessional summer, the earth's north-south axis was oriented toward the Milky Way, aligned with the plane of the galaxy, and the northern sky was illuminated with millions of brilliant stars. The great mass of stars clustered in that plane shed its influence directly down from overhead, highly charging the earth and all forms of life growing upon it. Our ancestors were constantly bathed in a shower of light and radiation, pouring in through their spines, meridians, chakras, organs, tissues, and trillions of cells. They became very highly energized, and their consciousness developed heightened awareness and capacities.

Not only was the human brain much more activated during that period, but also all the botanical sources of food were much more vigorous, requiring hardly any cultivation.

Cultures and civilizations around the world have myths and legends of gods, magical animals, and culture bearers who bestowed fire, grain, and other divine gifts on humankind and imparted the arts and sciences. In myth and later scripture, this era was known as the Golden Age and was peaceful and prosperous, healthy and wise. For example, the Roman poet Ovid writes:

> Golden was that first age which, with no one to compel, without a law, of its own will, kept faith and did the right. There was no fear of punishment, no threatening words were to be read on brazen tables; no suppliant throng gazed fearfully upon its judge's face; but without judges lived secure. Not yet had the pine-tree, felled on its native mountains, descended thence into the watery plain to visit other lands; men knew no shores except their own. Not yet were cities begirt with steep moats; there were no trumpets of straight, no horns of curving brass, no swords or helmets. There was no need at all of armed men, for nations, secure from war's alarms, passed the years in gentle ease. The earth herself, without compulsion, untouched by hoe or plowshare, of herself gave all things needful. And men, content with food which came with no one's seeking, gathered the arbute fruit, strawberries from the mountain-sides, cornel-cherries, berries hanging thick upon the prickly bramble, and acorns fallen from the spreading tree of Jove. Then spring was everlasting, and gentle zephyrs with warm breath played with the flowers that sprang unplanted. Anon the earth, untilled, brought forth her stores of grain, and the fields, though unfallowed, grew white with the heavy, bearded wheat.

Figure 37. Artistic representations of the Golden Age from medieval to modern times by Lucas Cranach the Elder, Abraham Bloemaert, and Andre Derain

It is impossible to date eras like this, but it clearly predates the historical spiral. Whether humanity's infancy and early childhood was truly golden, the memory or desire for lost paradise continued to inspire humanity's artistic and creative imagination as the new cycle of prehistory and history began (see Figure 37)

Awned and Awnless Grain

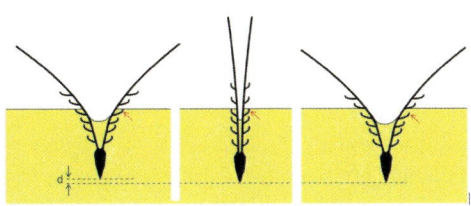

Figure 38. *Left*: Long, thin spiky awns of barley gather energy from the cosmos and concentrate it in the growing heads. When consumed, awned grains enhance intuition, creativity, and universality. *Right*: the awns open during the day (*left seed*), close at night (*middle seed*), and their rotation pushes the seed deeper into the ground, improving its likelihood of germinating (*right seed*)[40]

A key to this ancient peaceful era lies in Ovid's use of the term "bearded wheat" at the end of his tribute to describe the staple food of the Golden Age. "Bearded" refers to *awns*, the long bristles or spikes on cereal grains. Close up, awns look like facial hair on the growing heads or kernels of grains; hence the name "bearded." They may be short or long, single or multiple, curved or straight. Some grains like barley, wheat, and rye have long, elegant beards, between 4-7 inches. Others like millet are only 1/2–to-1 inch, virtual stubble. Awnless grains were traditionally known as "beardless" or "bald."[38]

Like antennae, awns gather and absorb the waves and vibrations of the cosmos, including the sun, moon, stars, and distant galaxies (see Figure 38). Although the beards are removed—or we might say shaved—during harvest and before eating, the high frequency energy enters and charges the kernels while growing in the field. When ingested as a whole grain or grain products, such as bread, other baked goods, noodles and pasta, and beer, that quanta of stored energy vitalizes one's spirit, mind, and body. Like William Blake's poetic image of holding "infinity in the palm of your hand and Eternity in an hour," the awns carry an imprint of the infinite universe.[39] At night, awns rotate and point downward, also absorbing the deep energy of the earth.

Besides allowing us to access higher frequencies of cosmic energy and develop higher consciousness, awns also serve a practical function. The tiny barbs of awns hinder mammals from nibbling the ripening grain and adhere to their fur for propagating. As the grain ripens and naturally falls to earth, the awns serve as rotating blades to drive the seeds deeper into the soil than if they fell flat on the ground. Similarly, during increased humidity at night, the bristles straighten vertically, twine together, and further push the seed into the earth. During the day, when the humidity drops, the awns open again, and fine silica hairs on the bristles prevent the seeds from reversing direction. In this way, the awns can propel the seed into the soil up to an inch, ensuring that more will germinate (see Figure 38).

For most of their existence, early humans consumed strong, wild awned grains. During periods of high natural electromagnetic radiation, when the Milky Way galaxy was directly overhead (e.g., about 15,000-20,000 years ago), the enhanced energy created an era of abundance and peace that was remembered as the time of Paradise.[41] Awned rice, wheat, barley, and other grains were a key to attracting, channeling, and storing this powerful energy. Meanwhile, as the constellations precessed, the Milky Way dropped in the sky and its energy diminished. Wild grains and other food grew scarce, farming began, and awnless varieties of grains started to displace awned strains because they were easier to harvest and process.

Unrecorded History

The arc that preceded the Spiral of History began about 12,000 to 13,000 years ago and lasted until the start of the historical era circa 3200 BCE. This prehistoric epoch may be drawn with a dotted line in diagrams because few if any written records or other datable evidence survives from this time. Broadly, this preliminary stage marks the transition from the Old Stone Age (or Paleolithic) to the Middle Stone Age (Mesolithic) to the New Stone Age (Neolithic).

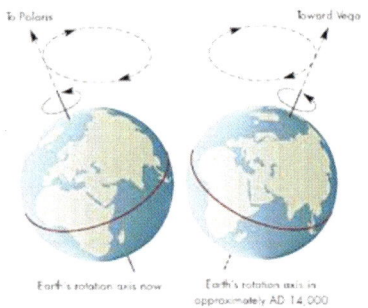

Figure 39. The oscillation of the North Star between Polaris and Vega over the course of 25,800 years steadily alters the electromagnetic energy reaching the earth

As the bright plane of the Milky Way relative to earth declined in the night sky and Vega rose overhead as the new Pole Star about 12,000 to 13,000 years ago, there was a fundamental shift or diminution of light and other natural electromagnetic energy from the heavens reaching earth (see Figure 39). Major celestial and terrestrial changes followed, including a massive comet impacting the northern regions of the world, disrupting human culture and civilization, and ushering in an era of darkness and struggle. These atmospheric and geological changes precipitated the melting of glaciers in Europe, North America, and Northern Asia and the start of an interglacial period known as the Holocene. In the era of transition to farming, as temperate forest replaced frozen tundra, hunting continued, and as the ice sheets melted, fishing again flourished. The bow and arrow reached complete development, and the dog was tamed to help in securing game. As the earth started to warm up again, settled human communities devoted to wild cereal grain harvesting began to form. Cultivation of grain soon followed, along with domestication of animals, and horses, cattle, sheep, goats, and pigs were kept in Eurasia and North Africa as a supplemental source of food in cold weather and for use during times of poor harvest.

The Mesolithic era began following the destruction of a large swath of human culture and existence between 12,000 and 13,000 years ago. Ancient myth and legend relate that there was a giant flood or series of floods in which most ancient cultures were destroyed. The Sumerian myth of Gilgamesh, the story of Noah's Flood in the Bible, and similar tales from China, Mesoamerica, West Africa, and other regions describe a great inundation from which only a few divinely chosen individuals and their immediate families, servants, and, in some versions, pairs of animals survived.

Figure 40. A giant comet entered the earth's atmosphere during the Younger Dryas geological era about 13,000 years ago, triggering climactic changes that contributed to the collapse of ancient culture and society

Recent geological, climactic, and atmospheric evidence suggests that a giant comet entered the atmosphere during the Younger Dryas geological era about 12,900 years ago and broke into fragments (see Figure 40).[42] Some of these impacted the northern hemisphere from Canada to Europe and Russia, generating enormous amounts of heat that vaporized ice caps, destabilized the earth's crust, and sparked a deluge. Tidal waves, earthquakes, and other earth changes, including a possible partial axis shift, submerged many areas, washing away millennia of human habitation and accomplishments. A second round of devastating earth changes may have taken place about a thousand years later. Tales of the sinking of Atlantis, Lemuria, and other legendary continents and islands may hearken back to these tumultuous events.[43] In world astronomy, this era is marked by the rise of the constellation Lyra, the Harp, one of whose stars, Vega, the third brightest star in the northern sky, served as the North Star. *Vega* is an Arabic word meaning "Falling Eagle" and appears to refer to the end of the Golden Age symbolized by this powerful bird.

Over the next several millennia, the survivors of this harrowing time and their descendants struggled to keep alive and rebuild human culture and civilization following the cataclysmic destruction by water and ice. In about 7500 BCE, Heracles moved overhead, and a star in this constellation became the North Star. In mythology, the Greek hero is celebrated for completing twelve prodigious labors. These glance at the era of hardship that beset humanity and a baker's dozen of qualities demonstrating artfulness and craftiness needed to overcome this challenging new era.

Around 4500 BCE, the constellation Draco reached a zenith, and Thuban, a star in its tail, became the Pole Star. *Draco* is Latin for "dragon" and represents the dragon that guarded the Golden Apples of the Hesperides, symbolizing wisdom, immortality, and the fruits of renewed culture and civilization. The reign of this star cluster over the next three thousand years coincided with a global warming trend that caused the glacial ice in northern latitudes to retreat. Over the next several millennia, civilization slowly emerged in the Aegean, Sumer, Egypt, the Indus Sarvasati Valley in Pakistan and north India, Africa, China, the Americas, and other regions. (An observation shaft in the Great Pyramid in Giza points at the region in the night sky where Thuban would have been visible at this era.) Domestication of plants, including cereal grains, beans, vegetables, and fruits, and of animals, including the pig, sheep, goat, horse, cow, chicken, cat, and dog, spread throughout Eurasia. Villages and towns gave way to cities and urban settlements. The wheel, pottery, silk, and other inventions and discoveries led to material advances, and the copper age was succeeded by the bronze.

Dolmens, stone circles, and other megalithic sites proliferated around the world. These megalithic structures have long been associated with funerary and burial practices. A new view is now emerging that these monuments embody a high degree of mathematical precision in their construction and advanced astronomical knowledge in their alignment to solar and lunar events and phases (see Figures 41, 42, and 43). It is also now recognized that some of these structures were laid out in patterns along lines of enhanced electromagnetic energy flow. It is believed that standing stones can transmit waves and vibrations across fields and forests like acupuncture needles placed along meridians of energy in the body to stimulate various internal organs. In some cases, the stones and monuments appear to have been used to collect, generate, and transmit natural energy and radiation between the sky and earth for use in farming, energy production, and healing. These sites often served as observatories to chart celestial motions and mark key events, such as solstices and equinoxes. For example, the Sun Dagger site on Fajada Butte in Chaco Canyon, New Mexico, includes inscribed spiral petroglyphs that are illuminated or cast striking markings during the solstices, equinoxes, and the major and minor lunar standstills of the moon's 18.6-year cycle.

Many stone complexes were the site of planting ceremonies, harvest celebrations, and other community rituals. They also encoded astronomical knowledge. In *Hamlet's Mill*, Giorgio de Santillana, a professor of the history of science at MIT, along with Hertha von Dechend, demonstrated that many myths were accurate representations of celestial events. For example, the story of Hamlet derives from an ancient Scandinavian myth of Amleth, a culture-bearer associated with the Big Dipper, or great heavenly mill, that churned the night sky and heralds the arrival of a new World Era.[44]

Figure 41. The cave paintings at Lascaux in France, the megalithic pillars at Gobekli Tepe in Turkey, and the stone circle at Nabta Playa in Egypt are illustrative of the sophisticated art and technology in the prehistoric world

Major archaeoastronomical sites include:

- **Lascaux** – Dating to about 15,000 BCE, famous for its Paleolithic wall paintings, the elegant murals in this complex of caves in southwestern France may constitute an ancient star map. The eyes of the bull, bird, and bird-man appear to correspond with the stars Vega, Altair, and Deneb known as the Summer Triangle
- **Gobekli Tepe** – An archaeological site in southeastern Turkey with ruins of more than 200 monumental stone pillars weighing up to 20 tons each. Dating from the tenth to eighth millennium BCE, the pillars include carved animal reliefs and abstract designs. Attributed to gatherer-hunters nourished on strains of wild grain, wheat appears to have been first domesticated near the site. Intensive wild grain cultivation and storage led to sedentism—the intermediary stage between nomadic gatherer-hunters and settled agriculturalists—and this stage of development appears to have given rise to the large-scale social organization necessary to create such monumental architecture
- **Nabta Playa** – A region in the Nubian Desert in Egypt that was the site of an ancient culture dating to the tenth millennium BCE that lived on wild sorghum, settled in planned villages, and

had deep wells that stored water year-round. A megalithic calendar circle dating to the fifth millennium BCE is oriented to the summer solstice and may also align with the stars in Orion's belt and Sirius
- **Old Europe** – A pre-Indo-European culture that flourished in Eastern Europe between about 5400 and 2800 BCE and had elaborate artwork, construction, and necropolises with spiral motifs and astro-archaeological orientations. Parta, a Neolithic sanctuary from the Banat (a region including regions of Romania, Serbia, and Hungary), had an altar illuminated by the sun and a small statue of a divine couple represented by the bull god and mother goddess. The necropolis at Cernica, the largest in the Neolithic age, dates to the fifth millennium BCE, and the dead are oriented towards the sunrise or sunset at the time of burial
- **Newgrange** – A massive mound in the Boyne Valley of Ireland, measuring about 300 feet in diameter and 50 feet high, dating back five thousand years. At the winter solstice, light shines along the central passage into the center of the tomb. It was built by an agrarian community and served as a spiritual and ceremonial center. A triple spiral is carved into a rock near the entrance of the monument and was incorporated into later Celtic culture. A recent theory holds that mounds such as this may have been birthing centers for expectant mothers in addition to serving as observatories and tombs
- **Stonehenge** – A ring of standing stones in the earthworks in the Salisbury Plain of England, dating to about 3000 BCE, that is aligned with the solstices and serves as a perpetual solar and lunar calendar. The site also incorporates the Golden Ratio and the spirallic Fibonacci Series (1,2,3,5,8,13,21,34,55, . . .) in its design. The site's main features are *trilithons* (standing structures consisting of two large vertical stone posts topped by a third stone set horizontally across the top). The trilithon glances at the first three numbers of the Fibonacci Series: 1, 2, 3. The next numbers are generated by the megalithic yard, a standard unit of measure equaling 2.073 meters. There are then 5 trilithons arranged around an oval whose short axis measures 8 megalithic yards and whose long axis measures 13 megalithic yards. The radius of the site from the center to the outer ring of *Aubrey Holes* measures 21 megalithic yards. There are 34 *sarsen stones* (large sandstone columns that form the external wall of the Stonehenge circle. The distance from the *Heel stone* pair to the southwest along the midsummer dawn axis measures 55 megalithic yards. As Neil L. Thomas, an Australian engi-

neer, concludes in his booklet *Stonehenge and the Fibonacci Code*, "The complete design of Stonehenge—every column—every linear distance—all are accounted for, nothing missing, none left over."⁴⁵

- **Kukulcan Pyramid** – A step-pyramid in the Mayan center of Chichen Itza in Mexico with 91 steps on four sides plus one at the top for a total of 365 steps, corresponding with the days of the year. On the equinoxes, a shadow falls across a balustrade mimicking a serpent descending the stairway with its head at the base in light. Most Mayan sites are also aligned to Venus, which plays a leading role in Mayan mythology

Figure 42. The earliest use of the Golden Ratio in art and sculpture appears in a multitude of animal figures in the Chauvet cave in southeastern France. The overlaid diagram superimposed on the rhino's horns was added to illustrate the proportion by Dr. Elliot McGucken. The art dates to about 33,000 years ago

Figure 43. New Grange in Ireland, Stonehenge in England, and the Kukulcan Pyramid in Mexico embody spiral ratios and principles and served as calendars and astronomical observatories

A common theme in ancient myths and legends, such as the sinking of Atlantis in Plato's account, is the misuse of technology, triggering natural catastrophes and an end of the Golden or Silver Age. Another familiar motif, described in Genesis, is that after the deluge humankind had to earn a living by the sweat of its brow and grow its own food.

Whether this era was enlightened and possessed a lost high technology or was lacking in consciousness and dependent on eking out an existence with only the most primitive tools, the archaic world largely disappeared in the wake of spreading glacial ice, epic floods, and other natural catastrophes. Standing stones, circles, mounds, and other megalithic structures and the secrets they may have contained fell into disuse, and many vanished beneath the rising waters, enveloping jungle, encroaching desert, and settling volcanic ash. Still, thousands remain today, silent witnesses to a remarkable lost heritage—the architectural counterpart to the ghost populations known to us only by traces of DNA.

Overall, this long prehistoric era—culminating in thousands of years of megalithic building—constitute the prelude to the Spiral of History. This epoch has been described as the Wilderness Era, extending from a time of great earth changes that imperiled humanity's continued existence, through a long period of hardship and survival, to the first stirrings of renewed community, prosperity, and harmony. It is to what we may call the Five Peaceful Civilizations—the bridge between history and prehistory—that we now turn.

4
FIVE PEACEFUL CIVILIZATIONS

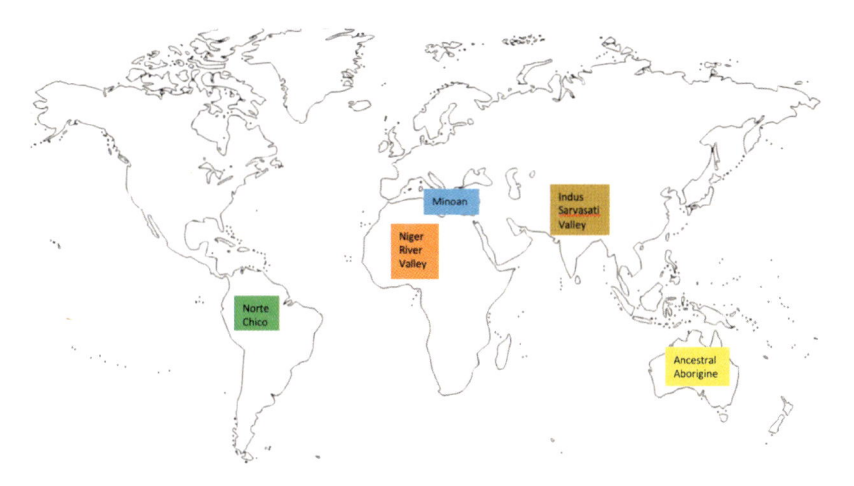

44. The Five Peaceful Civilizations

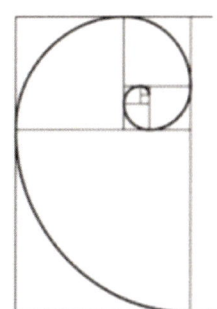

The Spiral of History unfolded in a peaceful, harmonious way with the gradual rise of civilization on five continents: Europe, Asia, Africa, the Americas, and Australia. Agriculture, proto-writing, writing, or symbolic communication, and towns and cities developed in the ancient Mediterranean, Indus Sarvasati Valley, Niger River Valley, and coastal northwest South America, leading to prosperous civilizations that endured for fifteen hundred years or longer. Australia alone never domesticated crops or developed writing, but its sophisticated fire-based natural agriculture and psychic means of communication led to a remarkably resilient social and cultural heritage that outlasted all the others and continues to this day. In all five of the early civilizations, the arts and sciences flourished. Families, communities, and large urban societies lived in harmony with their environment for generation after generation without religion and caste, rulers and priests, the subordination of women and children, and violence and warfare.

These civilizations, on the cusp of the beginning of the Spiral of History, provided continuity with the harmonious megalithic cultures of the past. They embodied early humankind's cherished hope that the balance of female and male energy, spirit and matter, and the practical and visionary that they embodied would prevail in the new era dawning around them. These five civilizations serve as a bridge between the prehistoric world and the unfolding new historical era.

1. The Minoans

Figure 45. Odysseus (*lower left*) washes ashore on the utopian island of Scheria. Painting by Jan Breughel the Elder, 16th century

In the Homeric epics, Odysseus washes ashore on Scheria, the island of the Phaeacians (no relation to the Phoenicians) (see Figure 45). During his terrifying ten-year odyssey, he loses all his men and ships on the way home to Ithaca from the battlefield in Troy. In contrast to the lotus-eaters, Cyclops, Sirens, and other monsters, as well as the sorceresses Circe and Calypso that he has encountered, the Phaeacians mark Odysseus's return to human culture and civilization. Indeed, the land of mariners is inhabited by a golden race whose main activities are dancing, fashion, shipbuilding, and navigation.

At a banquet, King Alcinous explains to his bedraggled guest that the Phaeacians excel in the arts of peace, not war:

> Our prowess . . . our skills, given by Zeus,
> and practiced from our father's time to this—
> not in the boxing ring nor the *palestra* [wrestling gym]
> conspicuous, but in racing, land or sea;
> and all our days we set great store by feasting,
> harpers, and the grace of dancing choirs,
> changes of dress, warm baths, and downy beds,
> O master dancers of the Phaeacians!
> Perform now: let our guest on his return
> tell his companions we excel the world
> in dance and song, as in our ships and running.[46]

After an evening of dance and song, the Phaeacian princes present Odysseus with splendid gifts, and the evening ends in a sumptuous feast. Sea-Reach, an impetuous young man who earlier offended Odysseus in a sporting competition, presents him a valuable sword. The wily tactician replies, "My hand, friend; may the gods award you fortune. I hope no pressing need comes on you ever for this fine blade you give me in amends."

Odysseus also learns that the Phaeacians excel in the nautical arts. But unlike contemporary Aegean and Mediterranean seafarers, they have no warships. In keeping with their harmonious heritage, they have only vessels that ply the seas for peaceful trade and missions of mercy. As King Alcinous reveals, the island's unique ships have neither steersman nor oars, but navigate by "divining the crew's wishes, as they do, and knowing, as they do, the ports of call about the world."

As his visit comes to an end, Odysseus tactfully turns down an offer from the monarch and his strong-willed queen, Arete, to marry Nausicaa, their plucky daughter and young woman who cared for him when he washed ashore. The Phaeacians graciously bestow valuable gifts on their illustrious visitor, including a chest of garments, gold in various shapes and adornments, and a bevy of tripods and deep-bellied cauldrons. The treasure helps make up for the booty from Troy lost when his ships capsized on the long voyage home. The Phaeacians then offer to transport Odysseus to Ithaca in a ship provisioned with simple loaves of barley bread and wine. In keeping with their Golden Age pedigree, no weapons, even ceremonial ones, are taken aboard ship on the voyage, nor meat or other animal food stocked for refreshment.

Reaching Ithaca after a blissful journey, the Phaeacians draw into a cove and run the ship's keel half its length to shore, glancing at the Achaean warships beaching themselves at Troy. Unloading the ship, they carefully conceal their passenger's treasure around the roots of a lofty olive tree. Then they move Odysseus, still fast asleep, to the olive grove and depart without waking him.

Unfortunately for the Phaeacians, no good deed goes unpunished. On their way home, an irate Poseidon, god of the sea, turns their ship to stone and threatens to send an earthquake and raise a mountain around their home port. King Alcinous recalls his father's prophecy that one day just such a tragedy would strike.

Disguised as a beggar, Odysseus returns to the palace and slays the treacherous suitors who are eating his wife Penelope out of house and home and conspiring to murder his son Telemachus. Athena, Odysseus's guide and the goddess of wisdom, whose symbol is the olive branch of peace, arranges with Zeus, her father and the ruler of the Olympian gods, to bring an end to the cycle of violence and retribution in Ithaca. After reuniting with his family, the supreme warrior fulfills a prophecy uttered by the spirit of the sage Tiresias in the Underworld. He undertakes an errand in the wilderness that leads him to renounce war and live a peaceful, agrarian life growing cereal grains.

Figure 46. Minoan fresco of an active maritime port, one of many throughout the Aegean and Mediterranean regions

Phaeacia nods at the Golden Age described by Hesiod, but it is not a fantasy island like most of the surreal places visited by Odysseus on his homeward journey. Life on Scheria closely parallels the culture of the ancient Minoans. Minoan civilization flourished in Crete, a Mediterranean island, located equidistant between three continents (Europe, Asia, and Africa), between about 3600 to 1600 BCE. A mountainous island with peaks extending to 8000 feet high and fertile valleys, Crete was settled by Neolithic farmers growing barley and wheat about 7000 BCE. Its towns and villages developed into a complex agrarian and mercantile society with multi-storied houses, lush courtyards, paved streets, and indoor plumbing and piped water. As a powerful, maritime power, the reach of Minoan civilization extended from Spain in the west to Syria, Mesopotamia, the Black Sea, Afghanistan, and possibly the Indus Sarvasati Valley in the east (see Figure 46).[47] Its superbly built ships controlled the Bronze Age trade in copper, tin, and other valuable metals, as well as grain, olive oil, wine, fabric, jewelry, pottery, and luxury goods.

In one of his tall tales to his wife Penelope, a disguised Odysseus describes his visit to the island: "There is a land called Crete, in the midst of the wine-dark sea, a fair, rich land, begirt with water, and therein are many men, past counting, and ninety cities." He also mentions the great city Knossos, where King Minos reigned and conversed with his father Zeus. The Homeric epics, composed in about the eighth century BCE, draw largely on myth, legend, and other oral sources. The Trojan War dates to about four centuries earlier, circa 1250 BCE, and Minoan civilization itself was displaced by the Mycenaean four centuries before that, circa 1650 BCE.

The monumental structure at Knossos contains more than a thousand rooms (see Figure 47). But there is no record of a Minoan king by the name of Minos, nor is it clear whether kingship even existed. The name "Minoan"

Figure 47. Artistic recreation of the monumental structure at Knossos, possibly associated with the legendary labyrinth of King Minos

was bestowed on this ancient sea power in honor of the mythical king by Sir Arthur Evans, who discovered and excavated the site in the early twentieth century. He took it from a much later Greek myth. The ancient Egyptians referred to Crete as *Keftiu*, which may be close to the original name. The palatial structures contain beautiful frescoes with leaping dolphins, soaring swallows, entwined octopi, undulating snakes, and other animals; and colorful lilies, crocuses, and other delicate flowers. It also harbored workshops for making ceramics, storerooms for grain, olive oil, and other staples, and halls for meetings and celebrations. The pastel frescoes vividly portray the natural world and daily life with an emphasis on fashion, sports, dancing, harvesting, and other joyful pursuits. Females played a key role in Minoan society, and the women are depicted as attractive and stylish. They are attired in embroidered dresses, adorned with flowers in their hair, and often have open bloues displaying their breasts (see Figure 46). Some figurines are suggestive of goddesses or priestesses, and Minoan art celebrated the earth, sun, and moon.

Minoan society shows a high degree of organization and wealth, but there is no firm evidence of monarchy, royalty, a central authority, temples, or a military elite. There is no archaeological, artistic, or literary evidence of an army, offensive weapons, or defensive fortifications. Nor is there evidence of war, battles, or social violence over the span of nearly two millennia.[48] This contrasts sharply with ancient Sumer, Egypt, Babylon, Assyria, and other contemporary city-states and kingdoms and with later Greek culture. These civilizations were characterized by an hereditary monarchy, priests and priestesses, a largely patriarchal social order, and the glorification of war and military conquest. There are beautifully wrought daggers, swords, and spears in Knossos and other Minoan sites, but these appear to have been used solely

Figure 48. Minoan women from a fresco in the "Woman's House" in Akrotiri on the island of Santorini (Thera). Their elegant, fashionable dress, hairdos, and exposed breasts were typical of the culture

on ceremonial occasions, as Homer suggests in describing Sea-Reach's gift of a sword to Odysseus after the farewell banquet. Ancient swords were also held up to the heavens or lodged in the earth to chart star motions and tell the time.

The ubiquity of the Minoan double-axe, known as the *labrys*, has been likened to the cross in Christianity and the crescent in Islam. It appears prominently in Cretan frescoes, pottery, and seals (see Figure 49). However, the Minoan double-axe is not linked to actual military use or violent death. It was the same shape as the blade of the hoe used to grow barley, wheat, and other crops on the island. In Crete, it probably symbolized the balance of female and male energy and glances

Figure 49. The Minoan ceremonial double-axe symbolized equality between the sexes. Its shape derived from a basic agricultural implement and does not appear to have been used as a weapon. As a symbol of the divine feminine, it figures prominently in Homer's *Odyssey*

at a butterfly (the archetypal symbol of change and transformation) and the female reproductive organs (a symbol of fertility, birth, and rebirth).

In the *Odyssey*, Calypso gives Odysseus a bronze double-axe to fell a tree to build the raft that will take him to Phaeacia and thence home. Later in Ithaca, the climactic contest with the suitors to win Penelope's hand in marriage involves stringing a powerful bow and shooting an arrow through twelve double-axe heads. The tool's shape and form (two complementary blades) suggest a yin/yang equality between the sexes. Learning to harmonize with feminine energy is the central theme of the *Odyssey*. After encountering the divine feminine in the form of Circe, Calypso, Scylla, Charybdis, and Athena, as mythologist Joseph Campbell observed, the mighty warrior purges his extreme masculine war ethic until he is fit to return to his wife, family, and civic life.[49]

The *labrys* is linked etymologically to the Labyrinth, which appears to mean the "Palace of the Double Axe." According to Greek legend, King Minos regularly sacrificed seven Athenian youths and maidens to the Minotaur, a terrifying creature half human and half bull. To slay the beast, which inhabited the center of an impenetrable maze, the Athenian youth Theseus won the heart of a Cretan maiden Adriane, who gave him a ball of thread to unwind as he entered the Labyrinth and then find his way back. From a energetic view, the Labyrinth symbolizes the twists and turns, dead ends, and ever-changing spirallic movement of life. It is the journey into the deepest recesses of the soul and triumph over ignorance, fear, and desire. From a historical perspective, the defeat of the Minotaur by a Greek hero represents the ascendency of the Mycenaeans over the Minoans. The Mycenaeans, the first advanced culture in mainland Greece, colonized Crete after the catastrophic collapse of Minoan civilization.

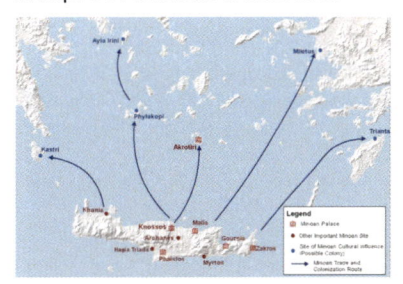

Figure 50. *Left*: Akrotiri (center island) on the island of Thera (modern Santorini) was the hub for Minoan commerce in the Aegean. The capital Knossos is in the top center of Crete below. *Right*: Artistic rendition of the massive volcano on Thera that destroyed Minoan culture and civilization after thousands of years

In about 1628 BCE, a powerful volcano on Thera, an island near Crete, erupted in the largest explosion in human history (see Figure 50). The eruption buried the capital Akrotiri, sent a plume of ash twenty miles into the stratosphere, and sparked a series of tsunamis up to 500 feet high. The explosion was preceded by smoldering emissions and other telltale signs, so the Minoans were able to evacuate before the eruption. Loss of life on Crete, which received the brunt of the tidal waves, was also minimal. However, the monumental building at Knossos, as well as most standing structures, were destroyed along with most of the fleet. There was a brief recovery and partial reconstruction, but within fifty years, Crete was colonized by the Mycenaeans, a martial culture from the Greek mainland. The glorious Minoan

Golden Age vanished, to be remembered only in myth and legend.

The catastrophic event on Thera is alluded to in the *Odyssey* when the Phaeacian vessel that transports Odysseus home is turned to stone and Poseidon threatens to bury the island under a mountain. The Greek warrior had incurred the wrath of Poseidon, the god of the sea, by maiming his son Polyphemus, the one-eyed Cyclops, and the sea god vowed vengeance. Volcanoes with their circular craters may have been personified as "one-eyed" monsters, or Cyclopses.

At the Phaeacian court, Odysseus learns that the inhabitants migrated to their island paradise after the cannibalistic Cyclopses tormented them in their original country. In the *Odyssey*, Phaeacia appears to be a colony established by Minoans fleeing the huge volcanic eruption and its aftermath. The Minotaur too may hearken back to this cataclysmic disaster, as a bellowing bull was also an ancient symbol for an erupting volcano. Cretan bulls played a central role in sporting events, but unlike later European tradition were never killed. Minoan acrobats, primarily female, competed to leap on their backs.[50] The famous fresco of bull-leaping illustrates the Golden Mean (see Figure 51). The performer on the bull's back is situated at the balancing point that divides the composition into two Golden Rectangles. The ratio 1: 0.1618 also appears in Minoan signet rings and other objects.

Figure 51. A Minoan fresco from Knossos displaying bull leaping, a nonviolent sport popular in the ancient world. The acrobat astride the bull (*center*) is at the balancing point of the Golden Ratio made by the bull, comparing the longer left section to the shorter right section

Until the time of the Thera cataclysm, Cretan society honored women and very likely observed a matrilineal social structure in which inheritance and male leadership went through the female line. According to this view, Minos was not the name of a tyrant or king, but an office and the counterpart of the female civic leader, priestess, or votive goddess. The companion, a strong, virile young man may have held an entirely secular post, served as the Lord of the Animals, and ruled the afterlife like Osiris and other Mediterranean male divinities.

The Minoans' written language, known as Linear A, remains largely undeciphered after 5000 years, so much about the civilization, Europe's first, remains speculative (see Figure 52).[51] Historians and scientists theor-

Figure 52. The undeciphered Phaistos Disk, a Minoan stone engraving in the form of a spiral dating to the third millennium BCE, appears to be a perpetual calendar that could be used by mariners plying the Aegean and Mediterranean

ize that the monumental structure excavated at Knossos was a 1) royal palace (presided over by either a queen, king, or both), 2) a temple and center of religious worship and cultic practices, 3) a secular community center devoted to the beauty of nature and the arts, sciences, and trade, or 4) some combination of the above. In the *Odyssey*, Homer notes, "Daedalus in Knossos once contrived a dancing-floor for fair-haired Ariadne." This suggests that the Labyrinth was originally used for musical and artistic pursuits, perhaps bull-leaping. In a surviving fragment, the later Greek philosopher Empedocles describes the Minoan as largely a pacifist and vegan culture: "Not then with unmixed blood / Of many bulls was ever an altar stained; But among men 'twas sacrilege most vile / To reave of life and eat the goodly limbs."[52]

This section on the Minoans is a brief summary of one of several epic themes in my recent book *The Circle of the Dance: Achilles's Shield, Odysseus's Oar, Calypso's Axe, and the New Golden Age*. I had been working on it for years, but the final piece of the Homeric puzzle came into focus for me after a visit to Santorini in 2018 and walking through the excavations at Akrotiri. The Minoan site and its beautiful artifacts and naturalistic murals radiated a calm, peaceful energy in sharp contrast to the harsh, warlike subject matter of the Parthenon and other classic Greek sites in Athens and other parts of the mainland.

2. Indus Sarasvati Civilization

The Indus Sarasvati Civilization (ISC) (ca. 3300-1700 BCE) constituted one of the world's oldest, most long-lived, and peaceful societies (see Figure 53). Flourishing in the valleys of the Indus and Sarasvati Rivers and their monsoon-fed tributaries in present-day Pakistan and Northwest India, the ISC contained an estimated population of 5 million at its zenith. Its two major cities, Harappa and Mohenjo-Daro (excavated by archaeologists in the 1920s) were laid out in the cardinal directions with wide boulevards, clusters of mud-brick houses, artisanal workshops, and other commercial buildings, a sophisticated

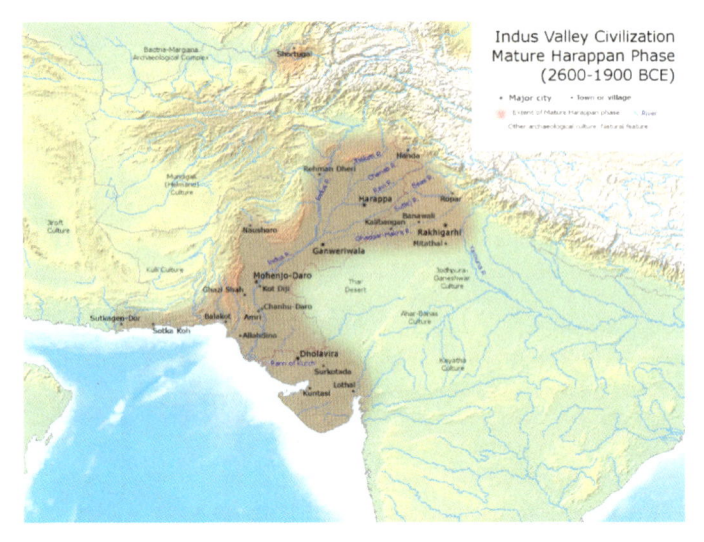

Figure 53. A civilization with millions of people flourished for nearly five thousand years in northwest Pakistan and India in the fertile Indus and Sarasvati River Valleys

drainage and sewage system, including wells, baths, and flush toilets in homes, and a thriving trade in handicrafts, metals, and jewelry that extended as far as Mesopotamia. Large structures, dubbed citadels by archaeologists, may have been administration buildings, granaries, warehouses, or public baths. Town planning made use of the decimal system, possibly the world's earliest.

Figure 54. Small figurine of the *Dancing Girl* (left) and the ruins of Mohenjo-Daro (*right*) where it was unearthed

All bricks and building materials had standard dimensions, and the grid-like pattern of urban development suggests advanced central planning. However, unlike Sumer, Egypt, China, and later Vedic civilizations, there is no evidence in the Indus Sarvasati Valleys of kings, priests, armies, temples, or palaces. Most structures were two stories or less in height. Dubbed the *Dancing Girl of Mohenjo-Daro*, the culture's most renowned artifact is a small bronze figurine of a girl or young woman standing in a naturalistic pose (see Figure 54). Except for a necklace and bangles, she is naked and has her right hand on her hip.

Bead making was a major industry, with jewelry and ornaments made of etched carnelian, gold, copper, shell, semi-precious stones, steatite, faience, and ivory. Pottery, featuring designs of plants, birds, and abstract figures, painted in black on a red surface, were another key product for domestic use and export. Timber, including teak from Gujarat, and copper from mines in Rajasthan and Baluchistan were major natural resources. The Indus Sarvasati appears to be the first civilization to use wheeled transport and boats. The bullock carts are indistinguishable from those still used today throughout the Indian subcontinent. Intricate canal networks, including a vast, dredged canal on the west coast of India, suggest the presence of sea-going vessels. Its extensive maritime fleet exported gold, copper, ivory, timber, and cotton to Mesopotamia, Oman, and Bahrain. Navigators used compasses carved out of conch shells to measure the angles between stars.

Figure 55. The Indus Sarvasati script (*left*) is predominantly naturalistic and geometrical and remains undeciphered. Hakra Ware from Mehrgarh (*right*) displays deer, antelopes, and other natural flora and fauna

The Indus Sarvasati Civilization also had an enigmatic script that remains undeciphered. The written language consisted of 400 to 600 distinct symbols on seals, ceramic pots, tablets, and other materials, including a sign over the gate of one city (see Figure 55). The symbols depict many geometric shapes, including spoked wheels and swastikas, and a zebu bull, elephant, tiger, and other real or imaginary animals. Some linguists speculate that the language may be a prototype of Dravidian, the major language family in South India. Another theory is that farmers from the Persian region of the Fertile Crescent introduced the tongue to Northwest India. Skeletal remains suggest a variety of ethnic types, including inhabitants with proto-Australoid features characteristic of South Asia, Southeast Asia, and Australia. There are no costly or conspicuous grave goods, as in the Mediterranean, suggesting an absence of social hierarchy and religious ritual. There is no sign of religion, temples, or priests and priestesses, and the art work, akin to that of the Minoans, is entirely naturalistic, depicting people, animals, and scenes from nature.

Mehrgarh, to the west of the Indus River valley, functioned as a main agricultural area since early Neolithic times (7000-2500 BCE). To the north, from Kandahar in Afghanistan to Baluchistan in Pakistan and as far as Iran and Turkmenistan, urbanization spread from about 4000 BCE. As in the Middle East, the principal grain in the region was barley (amounting to about 90% of grain consumption), followed by a small amount of wheat (10%). There was also a trace of cultivated millet and rice. Lentils, chickpeas, fruit, seeds, nuts, and other mostly plant foods complemented grains. Sesame was the main cooking oil with small amounts of linseed and mustard seed oils also used. Zebu or humped cattle were tamed for milk and meat as well as for leather and for pulling wooden plows. Sheep, goats, chickens, pigs, and possibly donkeys (but not horses) were also raised. Gazelle and wild sheep were hunted, and nets of cotton—the world's earliest use of this fabric—were employed to catch carp and other fish and shellfish. Traces of ginger, turmeric, cumin, and other hot spices suggest that curry dates back to this era. The kitchen in Harappan houses opened from the courtyard with a brick fireplace or hearth for cooking. Plates and ovens similar to modern day *tandoors* (clay ovens) have also been excavated. Dental remains show a generally healthy population, with significantly less illness than in other early urban states, and evidence surfaced of advanced dentistry.

The ISC appears to be one of the most egalitarian and peaceful civilizations in the ancient world. The absence of weapons of war, armor, fortifications, and evidence of battles, massacres, or cities set on fire (as in ancient Troy) suggest an extraordinarily prosperous, stable, and harmonious society. There are several skeletons of individuals who died from interpersonal violence over this span of several millennia, but none from battle. Arrows, spears, and knives existed, but appear to have used solely for hunting. No war scenes or motifs exist on artifacts (in contrast to early Egyptian and Sumerian engravings and Greek and Roman vases), and toys mirror peaceful everyday activities (e.g., tiny bullock carts and boats). Nor is there any sign of differentiation into rich and poor, slavery, or forced labor in the elaborately planned cities. Beauty, the culture's main preoccupation, shines through in its elaborate jewelry and fashion. Both females and males wore necklaces, bangles, and other adornments and sported elaborate hairstyles.

The peaceful nature of the ISC was echoed in the recent discovery of the Ban Chiang culture in northeast Thailand. Though much smaller, the Mekong River rice-growing society at this site was inhabited from about 2100 BCE for two thousand years. During this long era, spanning many generations, archaeologists have found no weapons or violent deaths. "The Ban Chiang skeletal evidence revealed that metal age agrarian societies in that part of Thailand were notably healthy and peaceful," observes archaeologist Joyce White. "There is no evidence for interpersonal violence consistent with warfare. The metallurgy was used for symbolic and utilitarian purposes."[53]

3. Niger River Valley Civilization

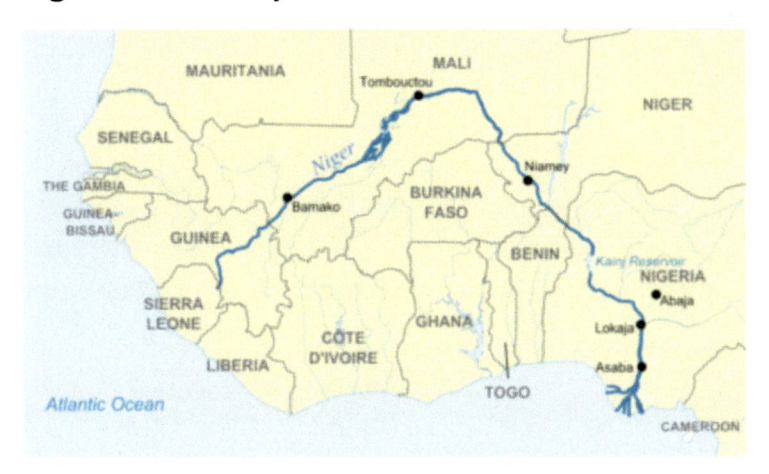

Figure 56. The Niger River Valley Civilization flourished in West Africa for thousands of years in a fertile region just south of the encroaching Sahara Desert. Its heartland was in Mali, later the site of Timbuktu (Tombouctou on the map), the great medieval Islamic learning center

The Niger River, the third longest in Africa, flows from west to east about 2600 miles from the highlands of Guinea to the Atlantic Ocean. Its circuitous route takes it northeast into the Sahara Desert where near the fabled city of Timbuktu it bends sharply southeast to the sea. West Africa, home to Niger-Congo cultures and languages, was a predominantly agricultural region and gave rise to one of the most harmonious and longest-lived civilizations in history (see Figure 56). Descended from the Niger River Valley Civilization, the largest ethnic groups of West Africans today are known as Mandé, and their roots extend back thousands of years.

Between 9000 and 5000 BCE, cultivation in the Niger River Valley (NRV) began, especially of yams, along with peas, groundnuts, and kola nuts. Palm oil was used in cooking, and wine was produced from palmyra, date palms, and coconut palms. The upper Niger River delta, a region of wetlands, saw the domestication of a native African species of rice. African wild rice, known as *Oryza barthii*, originally grew in the western Sahara. Once a grassland with massive lakes, the Sahara last turned into a desert about eight thousand years ago following a climactic drying trend, and the wild rice retreated to the inland delta where it survived in symbiosis with human cultivation and irrigation. *Oryza glaberrima*, the domesticated variety, did not shatter unlike its wild cousin, allowing for uniform harvests and a stable food supply (see Figure 57). From the floodplains, where it was domesticated about 1000 BCE, rice spread to the swampy areas of southern Senegal, and the entire West African rim, including Guinea, Sierra Leone, Liberia, Ivory Coast, Ghana, and Benin, came to be known as the Rice Coast. The middle Niger flood plain, the

96 Spiral of History

Figure 57. Wild rice (*left*) gave rise to domesticated African rice, a different variety than Asian rice. Until modern times, cultivated African rice (*right*) remained awned, with long, spiky bristles

most fertile region, comprised about 170,000 square kilometers, about three times as large as ancient Mesopotamia.

The intricate system of African rice cultivation included paddies, dikes, and transplanted seedlings. Seasonal rains, a mixture of highland and floodplain soils, and terraced elevations contributed to steady harvests and high yields. The principal tool was the *kajandu*, a long-handled fulcrum shovel with a flat iron blade used to prepare the soil.

By 400 CE, iron smelting entered the Niger Valley from Lake Chad and the Great Lakes along with copper trading networks. The fertile middle Niger floodplains eventually produced over forty varieties of cultivated rice, as well as sorghum, millet, and cotton. Used primarily for farming implements, the iron was of such high quality that it was later likened to steel. Fishing was also widespread, and the guinea fowl and other animals were tamed to supplement the grain-centered diet. Raffia, a type of palm, produced cloth.

Figure 58. This display depicts archaeological levels in the newly excavated city of Djenne Djeno in Mali where 40,000 people lived in harmony in a stateless society

The Niger River Valley consisted of small settlements or villages built on *tells,* or mounds, in between river channels and backwater swamps. However, there were also towns and cities, the biggest of which, Djenne-Djeno in present day Mali, numbered about 40,000 inhabitants at its peak between 250 BCE and 900 CE (see Figure 56). The city's urban center consisted of about forty mounds in a 4-kilometer radius. People lived in mud-brick houses and fished for catfish and perch as well as farmed and domesticated cows.

In the delta region, there were no monarchs, emperors, rulers, or other elites, and the citizens governed themselves peacefully for about fifteen hundred years. Nor were there any palaces, courts, police, armies, or even tax collectors. The Niger River Valley civilization consisted primarily of interdependent farmers and artisans. Terra-cotta pottery and statuettes depicted humans, antelopes, snakes, and other animals and may have figured in ancestral rituals as well as in domestic use. Skills and occupations were inherited, and marriage took place primarily within hereditary groups. Djenne Djeno was part of an extensive trans-Saharan trade network, exchanging rice and other food commodities for salt, copper, and dried fish. Glass beads from Rome and Asia dating to the third century BCE have been found at the site. Like the ancient Minoans and Indus Sarasvati Civilization, with which they partially overlapped in time, the Niger River Valley Civilization was entirely peaceful.

The civilization declined after 1100 CE, following the arrival of Islam, the rise of intertribal conflict and warfare, and the emergence of several large medieval African kingdoms. During the transition to central authority, key democratic values of the ancient peaceful culture served as a counterweight to rising despotism. As Roderick J. McIntosh concludes in *Ancient Middle Niger,* "Many aspects of Malian traditional society encourage norms consistent with democratic citizenship, including tolerance, trust, pluralism, the separation of powers, and the accountability of the leader to the governed. These ideas first appear in the founding epic of the nation [*Sundiata*], in which Sundjata Keita defeated a tyrant guilty of exercising illegitimate power."[54] In a later book of the *Spiral of History*, we will look in depth at *Sundiata*, the great West African epic, and West Africa's tradition of freedom, democracy, and egalitarianism prior to the East African and transatlantic slave trades. The epic was the inspiration for the recent hit productions of *The Lion King* and *Black Panther*.

Figure 59. Proto-Saharan, one of the world's oldest scripts, originated in West Africa and is similar to pottery inscriptions in megalithic Europe, the Indus Sarvasati Valley, Egypt, and Anatolia

Africa's oldest form of writing, Proto Saharan, goes back to Nubia (present day Sudan) and consists of inscriptions that resemble those for the gods of the Nile (see Figure 59). Egyptian hieroglyphs, known as *Medu Neter* ("Tongue of God"), dating to about 3000 BCE, influenced other early African scripts. Over the next millennia these included Kemetic (Hieratic), Thinite (Lybico-Berber), Vai (Mende), Wadi El-Hol (Proto-Sinaitic), Ge'ez (Ethiopic), Kemetic (Demotic), Coptic, and Old Nubian. In West Central Africa, an ancient script known as Nsibidi dates to 2000 BCE. Similar to Kemetic hieroglyphs, it was widely used to inscribe gourds, houses, textiles, and pottery. Tifinagh, a script created by Berber pastoralists in and around the Sahara, spread south, and ancient rock inscriptions survive in Niger, Mali, and other Niger Valley countries.

Though largely an oral culture, the Niger River Valley developed other symbolic methods of communication. Its distinctive art includes masks, metalwork, sculpture, and fiber art. Stylized human and animal figures predominate and include both abstract designs and natural shapes. A review of several representative pieces illustrates the spirallic historical changes that took place in the Niger delta and savannah from ancient times. Nok art, which dates from about 1000 BCE to 500 CE, emerged from one of the earliest cultures devoted to farming and iron smelting. Nok sculptures, including life size terracotta heads, were sculpted by hand from clay and gravel and fired and polished to a smooth patina. The iconic Nok statute of a man with his face resting on his chin in the Louvre in Paris (reminiscent of Rodin's *The Thinker*) dates to between 500 BCE and 500 CE (see Figure 60). Its angular shapes, perforated eyes and nose, elaborate hairstyle, and neck jewelry are typical of the period. The sculpture's enormous head may signify intelligence, longevity, or higher consciousness. The Nok sculptures are primarily of peaceful, domestic figures with elegant hair styling and body adornment and reflect the spirit of the harmonious, self-governing Niger River Civilization.

The Nok culture was located southeast of Djenne Djeno in an arid millet-growing region. The braided hair on Nok statutes bears an uncanny resemblance to pearl millet, whose long cylindrical spikes of tightly coiled grains

Figure 60. Pearl millet (*left*) was the staple grain in drier areas of Mali and West Africa. The Nok statue (*center*) and grand mosque in Timbuctu (right) were highly influenced by its color, energy, and vibrations

point vertically and reach up to 50 inches in length. The millet also bears a striking resemblance in conical shape, porous density, and sandy coloration to the architecture of the Grand Mosque in Timbuktu, the great medieval center of learning that flourished a thousand years later after the arrival of Islam and decline of traditional Niger Valley culture.

Masks traditionally played a central role in the initiation of children into adulthood, planting ceremonies, funerals, and other special occasions. The Bambara, the largest ethnic group in Mali, continues to produce a wide variety of masks. The main animal depicted in Bambara masks and headdresses is the antelope. Curiously, this wild creature is associated with the introduction of domesticated agriculture. In mythology, the antelope was the mythical being that taught humans to farm rice and millet. Today the *tjiwara* (wild farming animal) society continues to foster cooperation in the cultivation of rice and other staples. The Bambara hold masquerading competitions that recount the story of Tjiwara, son of the sky goddess and the earth god who took the form of a giant snake. Born as half-antelope and half-human, Tjiwara taught humanity how to sow and reap grain and other arts and sciences. The celestial goddess represents the egg and the earthly snake the sperm in this primordial Gondwanan myth. (Ancient Egypt also conceived the heavens as feminine and the earth as masculine.) The performers wear masks with upright horns, and their dances pantomime the antelope's graceful movements. The elongated and stocky legged body costume represents the aardvark that tunnels into the earth like a plow. The animal's high horns mirror the stalks of millet, and the dancer with the headdress abuts another dancer clad in long raffia stalks symbolizing the flow of water and a prosperous harvest. Males wear masks or headdresses with rows of zigzag patterns and curved horns, while females are adorned with antelope masks with baby antelopes on the back and have straight horns (see Figure 61). Offerings and libations of rice, millet, kola nuts, and fermented drinks are often poured over the masks. Giant wooden rice spoons carved in the shape of humans and animals also figure in some festivities.

Figure 61. Antelope (*left*) have inhabited the savannahs of West Africa for eons eating wild grains and other seeds. Tjiwara, the half-antelope, half-human culture-bearer (*center*), instructed humans how to grow whole grain rice and bequeathed other arts and sciences. Traditional antelope dances (*right*) continue to honor Tjiwara. Note how males wear an antelope headdress with curved horns, while females sport one with straight horns and a baby antelope on their backs

The antelope myth reflects more than just the transition from a Paleolithic gatherer-hunter society to a Neolithic farming society. Like its cousin, the gazelle, the antelope, a gentle, peaceful animal native to the African savanna, eats grass, shoots, and seeds. Its leaping ability and nonhierarchical social structure resist domestication. Females typically give birth to a single calf (and occasionally twins). All of these proto-human antelope qualities are incorporated into the peaceful, plant-based Niger River Valley Civilization.

In West Africa, God was called Bemba and, as in other Gandwanan myths, is a distant, abstract creator. One of his manifestations is Faro, an androgynous being, who is identified with water, light, speech, and light. Faro created humans from mud and wood into which he breathed life. As there was no concept of private ownership of land, Faro owned all the forests and fields. His representatives, the elders, administered it in his name in consultation with the ancestors and then lent it to families for personal use. Djenne Djeno, the hub of this remarkable civilization with tens of thousands of inhabitants, operated on the basis of natural law for scores of generations without central authority, monarchs, religion, a police force, or a military. (*Faro*, the supreme West African deity, shares a similar pronunciation and attributes of *Pharaoh*, the Egyptian monarch who embodied the deity Re, the personification of the creator and the sun. In the next volume of *Spiral of History*, we shall examine this link and the sub-Saharan origins of Egyptian civilization.)

Figure 62. Advanced metallurgy in West Africa goes back millennia and was used for making farming and cooking implements, jewelry, and other peaceful objects. Blacksmiths (like the contemporary one in the picture) traditionally served as spiritual guides and masters of *nyama* or natural electromagnetic energy

In Mali, the spiritual force, or energy of the cosmos, is known as *nyama*, akin to *qi* in China, *ka* in Egypt, or *pneuma* in Greece. Everything has *nyama*—people, animals, rocks, mountains, rivers, and seas. But usually only *nyamakalaw*, or skilled practitioners can shape and mold it into sublime art or harness its magical powers. Traditionally, *nyamakalaw* consisted of hereditary castes of blacksmith, healers, sorcerers, carpenters, and *griots* or bards. As McIntosh explains, "A central concept to all this is *nyama*, the vital force that permeates the entire Middle Niger (and the larger Mandé) landscape. *Nyama* permeates places; it can be harvested, but it can also be augmented by the (entrepreneurial) acts of leaders and specialists. Indeed, to be a blacksmith is only 20 percent about making iron and fully 80 percent about generating new volumes of *nyama* by the highly skilled, dangerous, and transformative act of setting earth to fire and extracting metal." (See figure 62.)

Figure 63. *Left*: The perspective and faces in Picasso's *Les Demoiselles d'Avignon* introducing Cubism were based on an African mask of Tjiwara. *Right*: A timeless scene of a small skiff making its way along the Niger River

"To be human in Mandé means to gain knowledge about the unequal flow and curation of *nyama* across this highly charged landscape," as McIntosh continues. "Some elect never to tempt the dangerous forces—they live lives of quiet mediocrity. Others, however, accept the role of authority that is to gather or manipulate *nyama* for the purpose of maintaining social and occult harmony in the world. These are the Heroes and Heroines, Men and Women of Crises, of the vast Mandé epics [such as] *Sundiata*."[55] As we shall see in the *Spiral of History* volume on the Modern World, a young Spanish painter named Pablo Picasso came across a traditional mask of Tjiwara, the antelope divinity, in a museum exhibit. The stunning creation led him to a multidimensional view of the world. He went on to invent Cubism, and the face of modern art was changed forever (see Figure 63).

4. Norte Chico Civilization

Figure 64. A panoramic view of the great earth pyramids at Caral, the hub of the earliest civilization in the Americas

Norte Chico, the earliest civilization in the Western Hemisphere, arose in the fourth millennium BCE in coastal north-central Peru. In three small valleys north of present-day Lima, the Norte Chico civilization occupied an area of nearly 700 square miles and included as many as thirty population centers (see Figure 64). The communities were fed by alluvial irrigation canals and surrounded by verdant wild lands with deer, vicuna, and birds with bright plumage. Monumental architecture, including terraced pyramids, an amphitheater, and standing stones, dotted the site and reached as high as 85

Figure 65. Norte Chico is in central Peru and dates to the fourth millennium BCE

feet. Caral, the main city, flourished from about 3500 to 1800 BCE. Norte Chico was ultimately displaced by rising cultures and population centers along the Peruvian coast and the Pacific side of the Andes (see Figure 65). Six enormous platform mounds at the site of Caral in the Supe Valley of the Andes represent the earliest human monuments in the Americas. In addition to the inland communities, there were major coastal settlements. Each of the thirteen inland centers had rectangular terraced pyramids, ranging from 105,000 to 196,000 cubic yards in volume. The sites also contained sunken circular plazas, smaller rounds, and residences and are laid out in spirals and other geometric patterns (see Figure 66).

Enjoying a mixed agricultural and maritime economy, the Norte Chico inhabitants lived primarily on quinoa, beans, squash, sweet potatoes, avocado, and other plant foods. Gourds were used for storage, and food was cooked with hot rocks heated in a fire pit, covered with stones, dirt, and leaves, and allowed to roast. A small amount of maize, originating in Central America, was also consumed as a secondary grain. Guava was a favorite fruit. Fisherfolk harvested many varieties of fish and shellfish, including anchovies, sardines, clams, and mussels. The society's agriculture was irrigation-based, fed by more than fifty rivers carrying snowmelt from the surrounding Andes.

The residents lived in dwellings made of adobe or of wood poles, cane, and mud. Excavations, which only began in the late 1990s and early 2000s, have not yet established whether there were workshops, marketplaces, or other signs of commercial activities. Dried anchovies may have served as currency. Caral had an extensive trade network, exporting its own products and importing shells from the Ecuador coast, dyes from the highlands of the Andes, and snuff from the Amazon.

As a pre-ceramic culture, Norte Chico lacked pottery and had virtually no graphic art. However, there were necklaces, pendants, brooches, and other adornments made of shells or bone that feature bird and animal motifs. Numerous flutes carved from pelican bone and trumpets from llama bone

Figure 66. The monumental architecture at Caral featured large earth pyramids (*left*) and standing stones arranged in circles, spirals, and other geometrical figures (*right*)

have survived, and the enormous vertebrae of the blue whale were used to make stools. The Norte Chicoans had a sophisticated textile technology and wove three distinct colors of cotton, as well as reeds and wild cane, into ropes and bags to assist in transporting quarried stone and river rocks to construction sites and to make fishing nets and clothing. For writing and communication, the culture used *quipu*, the system of knotted strings or cords made from alpaca and llama hairs, and used extensively by the much later Inkas for accounting and possibly for recording stories and music (see Figure 67).

While large-scale social organization and cooperation would have been necessary to build the monumental terraced pyramids, it is unclear to what degree there was a central authority, civic or religious. An image dubbed the Staff God, a hooded figure with large incisors, was unearthed on a single gourd. The figure appears to be an early version of Virachoca, the creator in later Inkan mythology. Females were buried or mummified similar to males, suggesting gender equality.

Figure 67. *Left*: the earliest known quipu (knotted string) in South America. *Right*: a carved fisherman in a traditional *totora*, or reed watercraft, dates to this early era

According to scientists, there is no archaeological sign of weapons or warfare of any kind at any excavated level during the entire period, spanning nearly two millennia. This absence includes no evidence of violent deaths, burned buildings, or other signs of conflict, and the architecture and layout of cities and settlements is completely non-defensive. This harmonious civilization contrasts sharply with later Andean societies, especially the vast Inkan

Empire, the best known, that were extraordinarily coercive, violent, and warlike.

5. Aboriginal Australia

Figure 68. A modern map of Australia with traditional Ancestral Aboriginal coloration, spiral symbols, and other motifs

Australia, the last continent to be colonized by Europeans, is also one of the oldest inhabited places on earth (see Figure 68). Native people, known as ancestral Aboriginals, have lived in Australia and the Torres Strait Islands for 65,000 to 100,000 years or more. DNA evidence suggests they descended from an early wave of Sapiens to leave Africa and travel through South and Southeast Asia to New Guinea which was then connected to Australia by a land bridge. They also have a small amount of DNA from Denisovans, an early hominin line that had a common ancestor with Neanderthals. Boats and rafts may also have been used for some passages. Australia is home to the world's earliest rock paintings, axes, breadmaking, and ritual cremation. At the time of European contact in 1788, 500 population groups occupied the continent with many distinctive traditions, languages, and practices (see Figure 69).

Figure 69. Engraving of the arrival of English ships to Australia in the 18th century

"[The natives] appear to be in reality far happier than we Europeans; being wholly unacquainted not only with the superfluous but the necessary Conveniences so much sought after in Europe, they are happy in not knowing the use of them," observed British explorer Captain James Cook. "They live in Tranquility which is not disturbed by the inequality of Condition: the Earth and sea of their own accord furnishes them with all things necessary for life, they covet not Magnificent Houses, Household-stuff, etc., they live in warm and fine Climate and enjoy a very wholesome Air, so that they have very little need of Clothing. . . . In short, they seemed to set no Value upon anything we gave them."[56]

About 1 million people lived in Australia at the time of initial contact. Unique among major human cultures and civilizations, the Aboriginals eschewed material development for artistic and spiritual realization. They lived in a timeless landscape that saw all life on earth as the manifestation on the eternal Dreamtime (*Alcheringa*) of the creative ancestral spirits. Indigenous people lived simply, mostly outdoors, though occasionally in bark shelters, caves, stilted huts, or windbreaks, and followed a semi-nomadic existence. They foraged wild foods, assembled during elaborate kinship and intertribal ceremonies and rituals, and sculpted the environment into an earthly paradise. In the Torres Strait Islands, they lived in permanent villages, and on the mainland semi-permanent fishing villages dotted the coastline. Along rivers, lakes, and flood plains, there are thousands of low oval or circular mounds that were used primarily as communal earth ovens. The mounds were typically 30–40 meters in diameter and less than 1 meter high and enclosed pits in which reeds, wild grains and herbs, and animal food were cooked over heated stones or burning clay lumps. In some cases, the mounds also likely served as the site of villages and the production of twine and nets.

Unlike cultures and civilizations on other continents, ancestral Aboriginals never developed farming, architecture, writing, and metallurgy. Instead, their cultural arc embraced a life of shared natural abundance, art, dance, song, and other aesthetic and spiritual pursuits. They fashioned wooden, fiber, and stone implements and tools, hunted and slept with the dingo (a semi-domesticated dog), and engaged in long-distance exchange. They also made objects of animal parts such as water-tight bags from kangaroo skin and sewing needles from bone. Artistic creations included ceremonial poles, figurines of mythic beings, ochre paintings on sheets of bark, and engravings on rock, in caves, and on sand. Music was made with the *didjeridu* (a long wooden trumpet), *bullroarer* (a wooden slat whirled around with a cord), *clapping sticks* (oval sticks painted with birds and animals), and the *gumleaf* (a Eucalyptus tree leaf that is blown on). Accomplished navigators, the Aboriginal Australians traveled in bark canoes, rafts, and dugout log canoes, including some with woven sails. New Zealand, a thousand miles distant, was settled by Polynesians in the thirteen century CE and, despite the proximity, had no contact with its larger continental neighbor to the west.

Aboriginal society was classless and had no chiefs, royalty, nobility, or centralized institutions of government. Generally egalitarian in matters of sexuality and gender, native Australian men and women shared in food preparation, child rearing, storytelling, painting, and other daily pursuits. Each sex had its own rituals and practices, and elders of both sexes exercised a strong influence on community decisions. The basic social unit was the family that camped and cooked together and was generally self-sufficient. Several families formed a band. Many bands in a region constituted estate groups that oversaw large regions and developed complex kinship networks. Although there was no private ownership of land, collective responsibility for maintaining sacred sites and territory usually descended through patrilineal descent. Males enjoyed more marriage rights, tended to dominate in councils, and could be abusive to their wives and daughters.[57] Across the continent, there is no evidence of war, but there was occasional group violence, light or mock combat to settle individual and clan disputes, capital punishment, and sporadic massacres. Weapons included spearthrowers, shields, boomerangs, and clubs. When Sydney was founded, a group of several hundred warriors gathered to confront the English but withdrew in the face of their superior firepower.

Use of Fire

Figure 70. *Aborigines Using Fire to Hunt Kangaroos* by Joseph Lycett (ca. 1817) portrays the innovative use of fire to transform the landscape and secure both animal and plant food

When Europeans arrived in Australia in the eighteenth century, as Captain Cook observed, they marveled at three main things: 1) the peacefulness and self-reliance of the native people, 2) the natural beauty of the land that appeared like a heavenly garden or royal estate, and 3) the primitive technology of the native inhabitants. Over the next three centuries, as disease, expropriation of native lands, and policies of extermination nearly wiped out the original population, it rarely occurred to the European arrivals that the majestic splendor of the continent was not natural but landscaped over the millennia.

The Aborigines did not have the compass, wheel, draft animals, writing, or metallurgy. But they had something much more creative and powerful. They had fire and they knew how to use it. In the course of endless generations, they transformed much of the bush—or forest—scrub, heath, tundra, beaches, and deserts—into carefully managed preserves for living, tending wild plants, and herding wild animals (see Figure 70). The secret was the selective use of fire to shape their surroundings. Contrary to conventional modern wisdom, outdoor fires are largely beneficial to the environment. Seeds of many species of plants need a high degree of heat to germinate. Fires also produce mineral-rich ash that fertilizes the soil.

Controlled Aboriginal fires ranged from limited scorchings in a relatively small space and over a short period of time (known as "cool fires") to large blazes over a wide territory and during a longer period of time (known as "hot fires"). There were many types, degrees, and hues in between, including multiple fires, line fires, and circle fires. Fires could be put out by fire keepers wielding dry branches, by anticipated rainfall (predicted, for example, by the movement of white ants carrying their eggs from river beds to higher ground), or by fire itself (fighting fire with fire to rob it of fuel and oxygen and to create a firebreak).

Songs, dances, and rituals often accompanied the burnings. As one Arnheim man explained, "You sing the country before you burn it. In your mind, you see the fire, you know where it is going, and you know where it will stop. Only then do you light the fire."[58]

An estimated 70% of the plants in Australia requires or tolerates fire. For example, the bark of the eucalyptus heals the tree's wounds after a fire and revives what outwardly appears to be a dead organism. Over the ages, native people learned how each species, as well as whole ecosystems, thrived and carefully controlled the ratio of plants, animals, and the natural food supply. Each of the continent's thousands of herbs, tubers, bulbs, and annuals required a different burning at different intensities and at different seasons. Hard seeds, pods, and legumes required hot fires to open. Burning every two to four years maintained perennial grasslands, while cool fires every two to three years kept the forest canopies open (see Figure 71). Luxuriant grasslands with elegant stands of solitary or wide-spaced trees, tree-lined hills, and broad swathes of grass on mountain slopes could take half a millennium to create—evidence of visionary planning that compares with the cathedrals of Europe.[59]

Figure 71. Controlled fires can be "hot" or "cool" and be tailored to specific wild plants and animals

Fire was also indispensable to supplement the native plant-rich diet with animal quality food. It exposed undershoots, bulbs, and other delicacies that kangaroos, wallabies, and emus liked to nibble on. Another technique to round up game was for hunters to form a circle, a mile or more in circumference, while standing about 100 feet apart, and holding lighted bark. Gradually the animals were driven to the center of the circle and could be slain by clubs and boomerangs. According to anthropologists, the traditional Aboriginal diet on average consisted of about 81% plant foods and 19% animal foods.[60]

Fire and smoke also served to repel insects and reptiles, clearing inhabited regions of potential threats that plagued similar climates and environments around the world. The smoke from fires also constituted a continental communications network that could be used to convey messages from one clan or tribe to another.

As Bill Gummage concluded in *The Biggest Estate on Earth: How Aborigines Made Australia*, the original people managed the entire country with "breathtaking complexity." He quotes Yibarbuk, a contemporary Aborigine, "The secret of fire in our traditional knowledge is that it is a thing that brings the land alive again. When we do burning, the whole land comes alive again—it is reborn." Fire, Gummage concludes, "was scalpel more than sword, taming the most fire-prone country on earth to welcome its periodic refreshing, its kiss of life. Far from today's safe and unsafe fires, campfire and bushfire were one; far from a feared enemy, fire was the closest ally."[61] Following the devastating fires in Australia in 2019 and 2020, the government appeared powerless to deal with the crisis, widely attributed to global warming and climate change. Native communities and activists like Gummage proposed traditional Aboriginal fire-fighting techniques be employed and finally started to gain the mainstream ear.

Songlines

Figure 72. Songlines, or paths following lines of natural electromagnetic energy, crisscross the continent, facilitating travel, communication, and cultural exchange

Crisscrossing Australia were songlines that served as travel paths, as well as corridors for communication and cultural exchange (see Figure 72). Also known as dreaming tracks, they followed lines of natural electromagnetic energy and were customarily marked by special stones, rock or bark engravings, or other impressions. Trekkers sang traditional songs, danced, and told stories that referred to watering holes, desert shrubs, and other features of the landscape or night sky along the way. For example, a song of the spiral-shaped Rainbow Serpent (Wagyl) offers a map to the rivers and mountains of northern Australia that this primal deity is credited with singing into existence. Communal mortars and grinding stones were often left for the convenience of passing travelers. Other migratory families, bands, and tribes prided themselves on traveling on pathless journeys. They would often set off without any provisions, trusting in the ancestral spirits to provide food and water.[62] Songs and dances constituted the main items of trade and gift-giving. Exchange of precious stones, shells, spears, seeds, flint, and other goods also extended across the continent. Sporadic visits to coastal Australia by Malay, Indonesian, and other Southeast Asian sailors introduced isolated contact with the wider world.

Figure 73. Emu Dreaming, the largest of the Aboriginal star clusters, spans the entire Milky Way

Like other indigenous societies, ancestral Australians cultivated a special relationship with the heavens. The most spectacular Aboriginal constellation, Emu Dreaming or Emu in the Sky, spans the length of the Milky Way (see Figure 73). The head of the emu, a large flightless bird, in the Coalsack nebula next to the Southern Cross, attaches to the long body and trailing legs in Scorpius in the Southern sky. Curiously, the Emu constellation is defined not by stars but by the dark, opaque nebular clouds in between star clusters. Focusing on the spaces in between objects, rather than the objects themselves, is a common form of Aboriginal perception that extends to the natural landscape as well as skyscape. Various Dreamtime myths were told about the planets and other celestial objects. Among some communities, Venus and Mars are known as the eyes of Byamee, the Spirit Father. Such tales were handed down orally and transmitted telepathically, a faculty that continues today in remote Australian communities, but which has been lost in most of the literate world.[63] It appears to be the main reason Australians never developed a written script—they didn't need one! They did have *message sticks,* or wood etched with angular lines and doets, that served as proto writing.

Food & Health

Figure 74. Wild rice (shown above) and wild millet were the main traditional grains of the Ancestral Australians. Note the long, beautiful awns or spikes

As gatherer-hunters, the Aborigines ate primarily plant food, including seeds of wild grasses, roots and tubers, fruits, seeds, and nuts. Agricultural and food processing implements included digging sticks, winnowing and threshing materials, and wooden bowls for food and water. Principal food included several varieties of highly awned wild millet, rice, and kangaroo grass (see Figure 74). *Bush tucker*, as it is called, also included warrigal greens, yam daisy, lotus root, macadamia nuts, coconuts, taro, and fungus. Meat, such as kangaroo, emu, and crocodile, was consumed in small amounts on a daily basis and in larger quantities during ceremonies and festivals. Birds, snakes, honey ants, Bogong moths, witchetty grubs, and other insects rounded out the traditional menu. Maritime communities enjoyed fish and seafood, and meals were prepared over campfires or wrapped in thin bark and baked in ground ovens. The world's oldest bread, a loaf midway between pancakes and loaf bread, was made from wild millet flour.

Along the north and east coasts, fisherfolk used lines with hooks made from bone, shell, wood, or animal spines. In other places, people fished by hand, stirring the muddy depths of a pool until the fish surfaced or placing poisonous leaves to daze their prey. On the open seas, people went out in dinghies and sang to dolphins that would round up the day's catch. To escape the dolphins, the fish would jump into the boats.

Overall, the health of the original Australians was exemplary. As Queensland researcher Stephen Webb concluded in *Paleopathology of Aboriginal Australians*, "The general health of Aborigines was very good anywhere on the continent. . . . [It] was nowhere near as poor as it was among [the Europeans] who came to colonize this continent just two hundred years ago, nor did their diseases include the highly infectious ones carried by the new settlers and which led to the devastation of numerous Aboriginal communities."[64]

How the Kangaroo Got Her Pouch

Figure 75. The kangaroo, one of the marsupials on the continent, is a major culture bearer in traditional Australian mythology. *Left*: mother and joey. *Right*: traditional rock art

Ancestral Aboriginal civilization may well be the healthiest, most peaceful, and sustainable civilization in the history of our species. For several thousand generations, the many individuals, families, bands, and communities on the continent lived in relative harmony with the natural environment. These classless and stateless societies enjoyed the natural bounty of the earth, patterned their lives on the eternal Dreamtime, and cultivated a virtual heaven on earth. Songs and music informed their migrations, domestic relations, initiations, and healing.

Still, the culture was not entirely pacific. There are instances of capital punishment for serious transgressions and evidence of scattered Aboriginal massacres of other Aboriginals in historic times. Today, contemporary indigenous feminists are challenging misogynist elements of the Dreamtime tradition. Over the last five thousand years, male domination and other excessive yang tendencies increased as the Spiral of History climaxed. Material advances included the domestication of the dingo, improved stone tools and fishing techniques, increased trade, a more complex kinship and social structure, clusters of mounds for communal living and tool production, and enhanced population growth. However, these trends seldom led to lethal intertribal conflicts, and for endless millennia, there appears to have been no private property, division of rich and poor, slavery, pillage, and warfare.

What is the secret of this unique continent and people? From an energetic perspective, several factors stand out. First, Australia is home to most of the world's marsupials. In addition to kangaroos, other female animals such as wallabies, koalas, opossums, and wombats also have pouches in which they nurture their young. A baby roo, known as a *joey*, is the size of a grain of rice at birth and remains secure in the pouch for 120 to 450 days. Kangaroo meat was an important staple in native diets, and indigenous people absorbed some of the energy from this unique type of mammal. Though Aboriginal women didn't have a physical pouch, their childrearing—especially the unusual degree to which they kept their children close to their bodies—shares this marsupial trait.

Also, kangaroos are herbivores, living on wild grasses and grains, flowers, leaves, ferns, and moss. Their plant-based diet makes them gentler and more peaceful than carnivores. The most important wild grains on the continent that both kangaroos and humans eat are wild strains of awned rice and millet. The two native Australian strains of rice (*Oryza rufipogonand* and *Oryza meridionalis*) are higher in nitrogen, phosphorus, sodium, calcium, manganese, and zinc than cultivated Asian rice (*Oryza sativa*). In addition to higher nutrition, the ancient rice has long awns, or antennae, that absorb the subtle energies of the cosmos and contribute to deeper awareness.[65]

Like the Australian, the rice of West Africa was also awned, but cultivated unlike that Down Under. Both regions also shared an archaic Gondwanan mythological tradition, sexual and gender equality, and high regard for the feminine divine. In contrast, for the most part, Asian rice in historic times—in China, Vedic India, and Japan—was predominately awnless. These more northerly civilizations shared a Lurasian mythology, a patriarchal ethic, and a history of strong material and spiritual development, but also one with systematic violence and war.

Like the antelope in West Africa and other parts of the northern hemisphere, the kangaroo served as a culture bearer in southern climes. Indeed, the kangaroo found in the monsoonal woodlands of northern Australia is known as the *antilopine kangaroo* because of its similarity in appearance to Eurasian and African antelopes, especially the inverted triangular face. In addition to its gentle and caring nature, the kangaroo has springy hind legs, a vertical stance, and other proto-human characteristics from eating a diet centered on wild awned grains. When alarmed, the kangaroo will stomp its foot on the ground and, if attacked, box and kick its opponent.

A traditional Dreamtime myth weaves together these evolutionary, dietary, and spiritual strands to explain how the kangaroo got her pouch. Once, she and her joey were on a riverbank and came upon a weeping wombat. The old wombat said that it had been abandoned because of its age and uselessness. The kangaroo took pity and said that she would be its friend and went off to find the tastiest wild grass to share. A human hunter appeared and threatened to kill the wombat with its boomerang. Forgetting about its baby, the kangaroo rallied to the wombat's defense, stomped its big feet, and drove away the invader. In the confusion, the joey was lost, but the mother found him playing by a gum tree. Meanwhile, the old wombat vanished. Unknown to the kangaroo, the wombat was Byamee, the great god of the Dreamtime in disguise, who had come down to earth to find which creature had the kindest heart. In honor of the kangaroo's selflessness, he fashioned a *dilly* (all-purpose fiber) bag apron from the bark of a eucalyptus tree and fastened it around her waist. Turning it into flesh, Byamee told her that now she would have a permanent place for her baby when she went about her daily round helping the other animals. The kangaroo was delighted with the gift but insisted that the wallabies and other marsupials also be given pouches so their babies would also be safe, and so it came to pass.[66]

Commonalities Among the Formative Civilizations

Beginning in the early fourth millennium BCE, the Spiral of History commenced on a peaceful, egalitarian note. In five major regions of the world, harmonious civilizations emerged. With prehistoric roots in the archaic mother goddess era, the hallmark of Minoan, Indus Sarvasati, Niger River, Norte Chico, and Aboriginal Australian civilizations was health, peace, and prosperity. For generation after generation, over the course of fifteen hundred years or more, each society flourished tranquilly with material abundance, a high standard of living, sexual and gender parity, symbolic communication, and cultivation of the arts and sciences. The Minoan and Indus Sarvasati had sophisticated water systems, including indoor flush toilets, the Niger had elegant art and sculpture, the Norte Chico monumental architecture and terraced pyramids, and Australia a sophisticated fire-based natural agriculture. Awned whole grains served as the main staple of the diet in all cases: Barley and to a lesser extent wheat in the Aegean and Indus realms, brown rice and millet in West Africa, quinoa and maize in South America, and wild strains of rice and millet in Australia. A small amount of wild game and fish complemented this predominantly plant-rich fare.

Three of the cultures venerated antelopes or gazelles, the grain-eating animals closest in evolution to humans, as educators, culture bearers, and symbols of grace and wisdom. In West Africa, the antelope served as the main intermediary between heaven and earth and taught humanity farming and the arts. In India, the antelope figured prominently on seals from the Indus Sarasvati Civilization. The mysterious bull-like "unicorn" depicted in Harappan art has been linked to the white-footed antelope, the largest antelope native to the Indian subcontinent popularly known as the Blue Bull. The antelope also appears in a dazzling, wall-size fresco from the Minoan civilization (see Figure 76). The fourth great wellspring of human culture, Norte Chico, revered the vicuna, llama, and alpaca—three antelope-like creatures

Figure 76. Antelopes figure prominently in the art of Niger River Valley, Indus Sarasvati, and Minoan Civilizations

Figure 77. Antelope-like llamas, alpacas, and vicunas are revered in South America

that are agile, graceful, and eat grasses on the mountainsides (see Figure 77). The fifth, Australia, honored the kangaroo, whose inverted triangular face resembled the antelope, and which also ate wild grasses and seeds.

From an evolutionary view, humans may have acquired their physical bodies, sociability, and primitive toolmaking from agile, gregarious fruit- and leaf-eating bonobos and chimpanzees. But hominins may well have developed their higher consciousness, gentle temperament, and independent streak from the wild awned grains that constituted their main staple—a food shared by lithe, peaceful antelopes and gazelles frolicking in the grasslands. Of course, ancestral humans went on to master fire, cook their food, and develop many more advanced arts and sciences. But spiritually, as the West Africa myth of Tjiwara, the culture bearer who taught humans how to domesticate rice, relates, we are children and grandchildren of these graceful ruminants that lived in the savannahs where humanity originated. Even when ancestral communities migrated half-way around the world to Australia and South America, gentle, peaceful animals such as the kangaroo and llama that ate wild awned grains and resembled the ancient African ruminants continued to serve as messengers between worlds.

None of the five great early civilizations had classes or castes, royalty, central authority, armed forces, or engaged in military activities or war. Nor were they isolated communities that kept to themselves. Each traded actively with neighboring and, in some cases, far-flung regions. The Minoan and Indus Sarvasati Valley had advanced copper and bronze metallurgy and maintained far flung networks with Egypt in the case of the former and Mesopotamia in the case of the latter. The Niger River Civilization had advance iron technology and supplied trade routes across the Sahara. Norte Chico had an extensive maritime commerce with coastal Peru. The ancestral Australians in the far north exchanged material goods on a small basis with the Melanesians.

In West Africa, advanced smelting and smithing were harnessed to the service of hoes, plows, and other farm tools, as well as jewelry, ceramics, and other household items. The weapons on all five continents were employed only for hunting or ceremonial use. In matters of gender and sexuality, females enjoyed equality and shared in governance at all levels. Humanity's "first religious experience reflected the psychological bond between mother and child," as historian Gerda Lerner notes.[67] The earliest tools were for digging and foraging wild plants with children. In Minoan society, a matrilineal

Civilization	Minoan	Indus Sarvasati River	Niger River Valley	Norte Chico	Ancestral Australian
Era	ca. 3200 - 1600 BCE	ca. 3200 - 1700 BCE	ca. 500 BCE - 500 CE	ca 3200 BCE - 1700 BCE	ca. 65,000 years ago to the present
Environment and Climate	Island, coastal, maritime	Delta, flood plain	Delta, flood plan, Sahel, desert	Mediterranean, coastal	Mixed, tropical, desert, temperate
Rivers and Seas	Kairotos River, Aegean Sea, Mediterranean	Indus & Sarvasati Rivers, Arabian Sea	Niger River	Maranon, Huallaga Rivers, Pacific Ocean	Murray & Darling Rivers, South Pacific
Mountains	Ida, Thera volcano	Karakoran	Fouda Djalion	Andes	Ufuro, Snowy and Victorian
Staple Grains	Awned barley, wheat	Awned barley, wheat	Awned brown rice, millet	Awned quinoa, maize	Awned native rice, wild millet
Animal food (wild & tamed)	Lamb, goat, fish	Cow, goat, lamb, fish	Fish, poultry	Fish, seafood, llama, alpaca	Kangaroo, emu, insects
Sweets, Alcohol, Drugs	Fruit, honey, mead, barley beer, wine	Fruit, honey, fermented beverages	Fruit, palm dates, honey, fermented	Fruit, honey, fermented beverages	Fruit, honey, fermented beverages
Dwellings	Adobe with indoor plumbing	Mudbrick with indoor plumbing	Mudbrick, reed	Adobe	Lean to, domed hut, lava stone
Art & Architecture	Knossos, Labyrinth, murals, pottery, spirals	Planned cities, seals, pottery, spiral designs	Sculpture, iron work, jewely, spiral designs	Central plazas, pyramids	Rock art, Songlines, spiral designs
Economy	Farming, maritime, metallurgy, artistic	Farming, maritime, artistic	Farmng, maritime, metallurgy, artistic	Maritime, farming, textile	Natural agriculture, artistic
Writing & Communication	Linear A & B scripts	Undeciphered script	Saharan protoscript	Quipu knotted cords	Telepathy, message sticks
Women & Gender Roles	Feminist-oriented & egalitarian	Egalitarian	Egalitarian	Egalitarian	Patriarchal, semi-egalitarian
Medicine & Healing	Diet, herbs, music, dance	Diet, herbs, music, dance	Diet, herbs, music, dance	Diet, herbs, music, dance	Diet, herbs, music, dance
Dieties & Spirit	Possible priestesses	Possible animal deities or culture bearers	Faro, mother goddess, Tjiwara antelope	Possible deity	Byamee, Dreamtime, ancestors
Violence & War	None	None	None	None	Rare, sporadic
Destiny	Destroyed by volcanic eruption	Collapse from drying of Sarvasati River	Collape from Islam, horse, civil war	Collapse from drought	Still active despite ethnic cleansing

Table 4. The Five Peaceful Civilizations

social structure prevailed. The Great Goddess of Neolithic times appears to have presided benevolently, though largely invisibly, over Crete and its maritime outposts. Similarly, there is a tradition of female egalitarianism in West Africa and Australia. The social system in ancient Peru remains unknown, but egalitarian burials suggest it was similar to these other early civilizations.

While there is no clear evidence of organized religion, deities, or a priestly class, inscriptions, pottery, and other artwork in each culture suggest a highly spiritual orientation. Each civilization's art and architecture celebrates nature (as opposed to gods, goddesses, and other denizens of the supernatural world), harmonizing with the rhythms of fertility, lunar and solar cycles, the orderly change of the seasons, and periodic rebirth and renewal. There were few if any grave goods, animal sacrifices, or evidence of belief in a fearsome afterlife. Celestial navigation was important to the seafaring Minoan and Indus Sarasvati Civilizations. Later West African societies in Mali such as the ancient Dogon had a sophisticated knowledge of astronomy based on the double star Sirius.[68] The complexes at Caral and in many sites in Australia also are oriented to the heavens.

Finally, the earliest civilizations shared a common destiny. With the exception of Australia, they vanished without a trace and were not rediscovered until the twentieth century. And three of these sustainable societies ended as a result of natural catastrophes beyond their control. The volcano on Thera, the hub of the Minoan Mediterranean network, erupted in the greatest natural explosion in historical times, rendered life on the island uninhabitable, and led to the collapse of the homeland in Crete. The Sarasvati River, one of the two main tributaries that were the lifeblood of the Indus Sarasvati Civilization, gradually dried up and appears to have led to the collapse of Mohenjo-Daro and Harappa, its twin metropolises. The Norte Chico Civilization was peacefully eclipsed by sustained drought and other climatic changes as larger population complexes began to appear to the south and north along the coast with greater access to water. The peaceful Niger River Valley Civilization in West Africa succumbed to cultural invasion with the arrival of the horse, weaponry, and Islam in medieval times. The Australian Aboriginals alone among the five foundational civilizations endured to the present and then only narrowly survived physical and cultural extermination.

The historical eras that followed were, in many ways, the polar opposite of these peaceful, harmonious civilizations. The rollcall of great historic cultures and societies, including Sumer, Egypt, ancient Israel, Greece, Rome, China, Vedic India, the Maya, and Inka, introduced many wonderful inventions and technologies, created astonishing art and architecture, and produced enduring works of history, literature, and poetry. But at heart, they were hierarchal, patriarchal, and militaristic. The monarchal and religious elites that emerged to govern these high civilizations all observed a heavy, animal-food based diet, practiced slavery, and kept their subjects in thrall by a combination of brute force and religious fear. And all these powerful state or imperial dynasties ended violently or destroyed themselves through shortsighted ecological practices that ruined the surrounding soil, forest, or waterways.

For good or ill, their legacy continues to influence our own world. Within these great cultures, the flame of justice, peace, and love that prevailed in prehistory and among the five peaceful cultures was kept alive, now flaring brightly, now dwindling to an ember. And who knows how many other similar civilizations lay waiting beneath desert sands or underwater troughs to be discovered? In Book 2 of *Spiral of History*, entitled *The Ancient World,* we shall turn to the dawn of the new agricultural revolution in the Fertile Crescent, East Asia, South Asia, and Classical Greek and Rome. We shall explore the rise and fall of the great civilizations in these regions, including their art and architecture, their approaches to diet and healing, and their scriptures and epics. We shall look at the rise of patriarchy, the suppression of the divine feminine, and other arcing filaments that largely governed the Spiral of History through the industrial and digital revolutions and are finally receding today as the New Era of Humanity dawns.

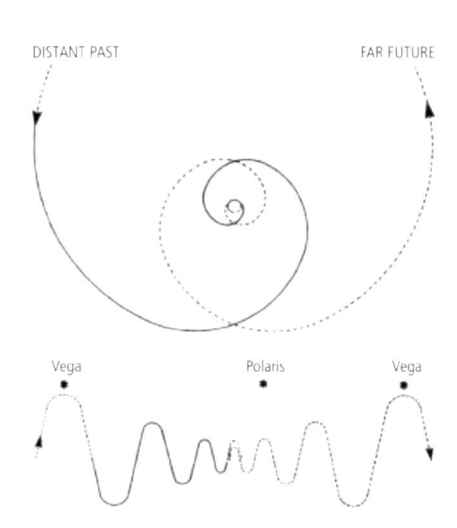

CODA 1: THE NEW ERA OF HUMANITY

Figure 78. 1. *Above*: The Precession of the Equinoxes moves centripetally over 25,800 years from the Distant Past to the Far Future in a series of alternating centripetal and centrifugal logarithmic spirals. At the end of a cycle, there is a transition of several generations before the start of the new cycle. 2. *Below*: Vega and Polaris alternate as North Stars every 12,000 to 13,000 years. The junction of the current Spiral (solid line) and the approaching new Spiral (broken line) overlaps from about 2040 until 2100. In the early twenty-second century, Polaris reaches its zenith directly overhead, coinciding with the formal beginning of the new Precessional cycle

As the current Spiral of History ends in the early mid twenty-first century, a short transition period of several generations will follow, leading to the formation of a bright new spiralic orbit that will last for about twelve to thirteen thousand years.

This new epoch, which we may call the New Era of Humanity, has already begun to unfold as the old era draws to a close. The relationship of these two spirals is similar to an Olympic relay race in which two runners jog together for a brief distance until the baton is safely passed (see Figure 78). When a secure hold is established, the new runner accelerates and takes off on her lap while the old runner fades away. In the human race—the contest to preserve, develop, and optimize our natural biological and spiritual quality—this period of overlap extends from roughly 2040 to 2100, when Polaris, the current pole star arrives precisely overhead. Like the full moon, its power and intensity build up slowly, reach a climax, and then dissipate suddenly (usually by the next day in the case of the moon). The two spirals will proceed in parallel until the new orientation is strong enough to lead and the old orientation decays. Realistically, it may take the momentum of the past disharmonious factors two or three generations to fade away. The first half of the new Precessional cycle, which begins about 2100, will end with Vega becoming the North Star in another 12,500 years. Thus, the full Polaris/Vega cycle oscillates between these two principal North Stars.

Destruction by Fire and Water

In many world mythologies, the Precessional cycle was associated with global catastrophes related to water and fire. The time when Vega last reigned as the North Star about 12,000 to 13,000 years coincided with a great flood or series of floods that inundated a large part of the world. As we saw, this may have come about as a result of the Younger Dryas impact event about this time when fragments of a large comet or asteroid slammed into the northern hemisphere and caused massive earth changes. The catastrophe linked with Polaris is one of fire. On a celestial scale, we are today just moments away from that catastrophe, as Polaris reaches its zenith. From a terrestrial perspective, we are already experiencing the start of that catastrophe as fire energy threatens the planet in many guises.

These include: 1) nuclear war, power, accidents, and waste that threaten to render the planet uninhabitable, 2) industrialization, including the spread of chemicals, plastics, pharmaceuticals, and other toxins that poison the planet, 3) global warming and climate change that overheat the planet and threaten life on many levels, 4) new deadly epidemic diseases similar to AIDS, Ebola, and Corona that may break out and spread worldwide without any effective vaccines or other remedies, and 5) chemical farming and agricultural genetic engineering that imperil the soil, crops, wildlife, and human health, and 6) artificial electromagnetic fields (EMFs) from computers, satellites, and cell phones that can affect DNA, increase susceptibility to disease, impede the navigational ability of bees, insects, and other animals, and generally disrupt living systems.

But perhaps the greatest fire tragedy of our age is simply the misuse of fire itself for cooking—the most ancient and basic of human activities. This abuse includes the widespread use of electrical, microwave, and induction (magnetic) heating that hinders or weakens the natural Qi energy of food. From the earliest cooking fires in Paleolithic times until the late nineteenth century and the beginning of the second half of the Spiral of Industrialization, (roughly 1880 to the present) all food cooked on the planet was prepared with wood, charcoal, hot rocks, kerosene, gas, or other natural flame.

Over the past century, electrical cooking, microwave, and induction cooking have emerged as principal food preparation methods at home and industrially. Food cooked with these methods can support human life and health to a degree, but over time it weakens our natural immunity to disease and clouds our consciousness.[69] Practically speaking, natural gas is the standard, most healthful way of cooking in the modern world (though some individuals react negatively in its presence). It derives from ancient plant and animal matter that has been exposed to intense heat and pressure beneath the surface of the earth. Over millions of years, this releases a mixture of gasses that can be used for cooking, heating, and electrical generation. Natural gas was first used in tiny quantities by the Chinese as early as a millennium BCE. Today it is used by about half the people in the world, but it is no longer sustainable. In America, it is linked with fracking and other technologies that are harmful to the environment. A new, more sustainable fuel will need to emerge if the worst aspects of climate change and global warming are to be averted. This may be solar, wind, hydroelectric or some new green technology yet to be discovered. In Africa and India, solar ovens are spreading rapidly and may be the wave of the future. Until then, natural gas can be used as a bridge fuel during a period of transition to a more sustainable planet.

Over the next several decades, modern civilization, which is based on dietary extremes, unsustainable economies, and flawed ideologies, will continue to decline and fall (see Figure 79).[70] At the same time, a new orientation is rising among those people who are adopting a balanced plant-rich diet, inclusive personal and social relations, and sustainable technologies. Through their understanding and efforts, the construction of a new healthy and peaceful world is already well under way.

The foundation for the new order will be natural and organic agriculture and farming, new renewable sources of energy and cooking, including transmutation of elements at low temperatures, the spread of yoga, taiqi, mindfulness, and other holistic pursuits, and psychic and spiritual development training. As the new orientation spreads, existing political, economic, religious, and cultural systems will be seen as complementary to one another and will evolve naturally as planetary civilization develops in a more peaceful direction.

If humanity is to survive, the safe start of this new spirallic age will probably lead to the establishment of a world federal government, or planetary commonwealth, to oversee the final abolition of nuclear weapons and other weapons of mass destruction. It will avert the worst aspects of global warming and climate change through sustainable food and agricultural methods as well as low-carbon advances in transport, communication, and other sectors. More challenging will be controlling artificial intelligence and big data, ending prejudice and discrimination, and learning to live together peacefully as planetary citizens. In this way, humanity's biological, psychological, and spiritual health and happiness can be secured naturally without resort to bionic and digital implants, artificial reproductive technologies, genetic engineering, virtual and augmented realities, geoengineering, new improved nuclear reac-

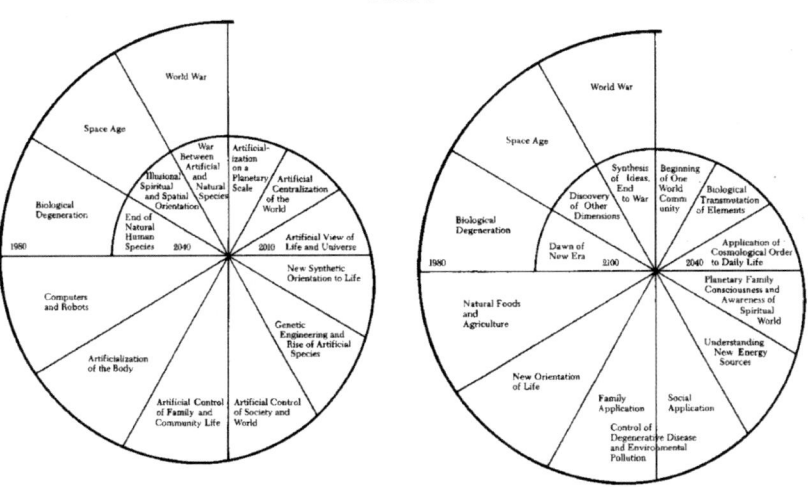

Figure 79. Choice of Futures: The end of the Spiral of History (*left*) from World War II to 2040 is governed by an accelerating material, genetic engineering, and artificial technological impulse. The Spiral (*right*) shows the overlap between the age now ending and the sustainable one beginning. Note: it spans 2040 to 2100 (60 years or several generations longer) and its orientation is organic, holistic, and spiritual. (Diagrams are from *One Peaceful World*, 1986)

tors, and other potentially unhealthy and harmful technologies.

The coming of Polaris, the North Star, directly overhead in about 2100, marks the end of the old Precession of the Equinoxes, the beginning of a new cycle, and the safe entry into the New Era of Humanity. If all goes well between now and 2100—a big *if* that depends on each and all of us—a new cycle of peace and unity will gradually begin that can be expected to last for many thousands of years as the celestial influence of the Milky Way increases. Of course, there will still be many trials, difficulties, and reversals along the way as various new North Stars arise overhead and guide us in our earthly journey. But overall, planetary energy will move in a brighter, healthier, and more harmonious direction. As the new era dawns, humanity will be poised to venture peacefully into the solar system. It will be ideally suited to encounter new worlds and spiritual dimensions and celebrate—for the first time as a unified species and planetary commonwealth—what Dante in *The Divine Comedy* famously called "the love that moves the stars."

Coda 2
ANIMALS THAT COOK: PROTO-COOKING BY MAMMALS, BIRDS, MOLLUSKS, & INSECTS

Figure 80. A chimpanzee uses a stick to extract honey from a beehive (*left*), a gull with a fish in its mouth searches for a hot rock on which to broil its dinner (*center*), and an iguana feasts on seaweed warmed by the tropic sun (*right*)

Humans are the only species that developed cooking into a highly refined art. But proto cooking and primitive food production are found among many other animals. Several species of fish, including wrasses, use rocks in the ocean to crack open scallops, urchins, and clams. Chimpanzees use sticks to extract honey from beehives and use wood or stone hammers to open nuts. Capuchins slaver their bodies with flavorful secretions from arthropods before eating them. Many birds chew and regurgitate their food as a form of pre-digestion for their young. They also catch fish and drop them on hot rocks in the blazing sun to warm them up before dining. Raccoons soak their food in water, and macaque monkeys wash sweet potatoes in saltwater before eating them to improve their taste.

Bees broil invading wasps or hornets with the warmth of their own bodies. Crocodiles and alligators stash their prey under water to decompose and bite off chunks when they are hungry. Bears and other animals seek out fermented berries. Crows drop walnuts from great heights to crack them open and in urban areas drop them on highways and patiently wait for cars to crush their shells. Iguanas on the Galapagos heat seaweed on sunny beaches to process them before eating. The crested caracara scavengers prefer charred carcasses of animals in areas of recent forest fires. Dogs bury pieces of meat because they prefer its flavor when it starts to decay. Parrots dunk their food in water before eating it. Even flatworms, nematodes, spiders, centipedes, beetles and other insects and small creatures inject enzymes in a prey to dissolve its body parts and improve its nutrition.

Recently, a troop of bonobos living in the Salonga National Park in Congo discovered how to use fire and cook their food, especially flying squirrels.

Kanzi, a bonobo in scientific captivity, was trained to strike a match, start a fire, gather wood from a distance, and cook food placed on a stick or a skillet.

In Australia, black kites and other large birds of prey known as "firehawks' pick up lighted twigs and brush from wlldfires and use it to set other areas ablaze and flush out smaller game.

These examples suggest a long line of evolutionary proto-cooking. Animals, as a rule, are instinctively afraid of fire. Fire burns and is hard to put out without arms and hands, though elephants can put out small fires with water in their trunks, and rhinoceros stomp it out with their leathery feet. A few animals don't fear fire. The frilled necked lizard in Australia is attracted to fire because it destroys the hiding places of insects and renders them into crisp, tasty morsels. Moths too are attracted to a flame and are notoriously at risk of singeing or burning themselves to death.

What accounts for these unusual animal behaviors? From an energetic perspective, fire is extremely yang—bright, hot, and active. Animals, especially predators, are also yang. Similars repel each other, hence wolves, lions, and other carnivores, instinctively retreat from fire. Opposites, on the other hand, attract. Moths are extremely yin, or light, delicate, and inhabit dark corners and crevices. They are attracted to fire, but unless they are careful may self-destruct.

As the center of the spiral of biological evolution, humans have strong contractive, or yang, capabilities, including a more highly charged midbrain and forebrain, highly developed thumb and index finger, and more compact teeth and jaw. But they also incorporate strong yin, or vertical qualities, including walking upright, a long digestive system that is suited primarily for processing plant quality food, and language arts. Grains, which drive these qualities and characteristics, incorporate strong yin and yang qualities in their structure and function. On the one hand, they are very compact or yang. On the other, they grow tall on stalks in the field that are very yin. While eating grains as principal food, human ancestors appear to have mimicked antelopes, gazelles, and other seed-eating animals and birds and developed higher, more complex consciousness. (The history and impact of the bird-human relationship is a fascinating subject in itself that will be discussed in a later volume in this series.) Hominins then went on to master fire, develop cooking, and fashion superior tools and technology. From stone, bone, and wood, they acquired skill in metallurgy, produced kilns (for cookware and pottery), and fashioned sickles, hammers, and other tools and implements.

As in the ancient myth of Tjiwara, the West African antelope deity who taught humanity how to farm rice, the other beings with whom we share the planet possess many of the same feelings and abilities as we do. Although they have largely been left behind following the Industrial Revolution except for meat and commercial byproducts, they continue to serve as culture bearers and wise messengers between worlds, and we ignore them at our peril.

Coda 3
Prayers, Meditations & Vizualizations
By Michio Kushi

Figure 81. Michio Kushi giving a spiritual development training seminar at the Kushi Institute in Becket MA in the early 1990s

PRAYERS

Daily Dedication for One Peaceful World

When we eat, let us reflect that we have come from food, which has come from nature by the order of the infinite universe, and let us be grateful for all that we have been given.

When we meet people, let us see them as brothers and sisters and remember that we have all come from the infinite universe through our parents and ancestors, and let us pray as One with all of humanity for universal love and peace on earth.

When we see the sun and moon, the sky and stars, mountains and rivers, seas and forests, fields and valleys, birds and animals, and all the wonders of nature, let us remember that we have come with them all from the infinite universe. Let us be thankful for our environment on earth and live in harmony with all that surrounds us.

When we see farms and villages, towns and cities, arts and cultures, societies and civilizations, and all the works of humanity, let us recall that our creativity has come from the infinite universe and has passed from generation to generation and spread over the entire earth. Let us be grateful for our birth on this planet with intelligence and wisdom and let us vow with all to realize endlessly our eternal dream of One Peaceful World through health, freedom, love, and justice.

Prayer at Meal

From God or the divine source, this food has come to us,
By this food, we realize ourselves on this planet,
To this food we are grateful,
For nature and people who have brought this food, we are thankful,
This food becomes us.
By eating together, we become one family on this planet,
Through this food, we all are one.
Let us love each other in this life,
Let us realize our endless dream.

VISUALIZATION

Visualization reduces stress and inspires hope for the future. Your daily life can then become the process through which you actualize this positive, healthy image of yourself, your environment, and the planet as a whole

Visualization for Healing Planet Earth

Sit quietly in any comfortable position and hold your hands on your lap or in the prayer position with palms touching. Stabilize your breathing.

Visualize the Earth as a bright tiny ball in the vastness of space.

Visualize that blue-green ball temporarily covered with a heavy, dark aura. Visualize the way of life and health spreading from kitchen to kitchen, home to home, family to family, beginning with you.

Visualize people gradually recovering their health as they eat and live in a more natural direction.

Visualize more and more of the land devoted to growing grains and vegetables and less and less to raising cattle and other livestock.

Visualize the rivers and streams becoming cleaner and cleaner as natural farming and organic gardening spread.

Visualize the air becoming purer and purer as less industrial pollutants and artificial electromagnetic energy from computers, cell phones, and other digital devices are released into the atmosphere.

Visualize the plants and animals thriving and returning to forests and woodlands, oceans and lakes.

Visualize human beings living peacefully on the planet, with no more war, crime, or violence; no more cancer, heart disease, viral epidemics or other major sickness; no more poverty and suffering; no more sexual or gender prejudice and discrimination; and no more injustice of any other kind.

Visualize people of all colors, sexes, ages, and backgrounds living harmoniously in a world of enduring peace, playing from morning till night, traveling freely, and respecting each other's customs, traditions, and ways of life.

Visualize the stagnated energy of the Earth from sickness, crime, war, climate change, and other sources melting into the general circulation of the energy as a whole. Visualize the Earth becoming lighter and more energized.

Visualize the dark aura of global warming around the Earth gradually dissolving, the temperature declining, and the Earth's aura—the ozone layer, Van Allen belt, aurora borealis—becoming brighter and brighter, lighter and lighter.

Visualize the Earth as a tiny ball in outer space surrounded by a radiant halo of energy spiraling through the Milky Way.

Visualize yourself as being at one with the Earth and all of life. Hold this image for a few moments, let it subside naturally, and allow your consciousness to return to normal.

Resources

Planetary Health, Inc. (PHI) An educational non-profit in the Berkshires in western Massachusetts founded and directed by Alex Jack and his associates. Planetary Health sponsors the Amberwaves network that helped prevent GMO rice and wheat from being commercialized in the United States and promotes organic and natural agriculture, as well as the cultivation of awned rice and other grains.

PHI also sponsors educational events, including the Macrobiotic Summer Conference, Online Winter Conference, and Spiritual Roots Retreat. Through its division, Berkshire Holistic, it is conducting a Whole-Foods, Plant-Based Dietary Intervention Study with diabetes patients in the Berkshires in conjunction with the Berkshire Medical Center, the region's principal hospital. Many of its activities are held at Eastover Resort & Eco-Village in Lenox, MA.

To subscribe to PHI's quarterly journal, *Amberwaves* ($25/year; $35 foreign), please contact: Box 487, Becket MA 01223 • 413-623-0012 • www.planetaryhealth.com.

Other PHI websites include: www.macrobioticsummerconference.com, www.amberwavesofgrain.com, www.makropedia.com, and www.ebolaanddiet.com.

PHI works closely with the Culinary Medicine School in Lee, MA founded by PHI culinary arts director Bettina Zumdick. Contact: www.culinarymedicineschool.com

PHI is also associated with www.gomacrobiotic.com, a website that posts many articles and videos on diet, cooking, health, and the environment. The site is hosted by Mariya and Vladimir Ivanov, Alex's daughter and son-in-law, who live on an organic homestead in Russia with their family and offer teaching, counseling, and other services.

PHI associates, including Alex Jack, also offer dietary and way of life counseling in person, online, and over the phone. Contact:

Planetary Health, Inc.
Box 487, Becket MA 01223
413-623-0012
alex@planetaryhealth.com

Notes

Overture
1. James Joyce, *Ulysses*, 1922.
2. This sentiment was originally enunciated by Theodore Parker, a Unitarian minister and Abolitionist leader in Boston during the era leading up to the Civil War. It was widely admired and popularized by Dr. King.

The Spiral of History
3. Thomas E. Mails, *The Hopi Survival Kit: The Prophecies, Instructions, and Warnings Revealed by the Last Elders*, Penguin Compass, 1997, pp. 209-210.
4. Arnold Toynbee, *Study of History* (the one-volume edition), 1972, p. 89.
5. As founder of the East West Foundation, Michio Kushi's convened the first conference on Diet & Cancer at Pine Manor Junior College in Brookline, MA in 1977, and it was attended by several people who had recovered from cancer using macrobiotics, as well as Boston physicians, medical researchers, and the general public. Michio met with Dr. Mark Hegsted of Harvard, who drafted the U.S. Senate's landmark report *Dietary Goals for the United States* that led to the first national guidelines. In the early 1980s, Michio offered dietary guidelines and cooking classes to men with AIDS in New York City when they were treated as outcastes and many churches and medical centers wouldn't welcome them. In the face of a potentially global outbreak, Michio issued dietary and lifestyle guidelines for the Ebola epidemic in West Africa in 2014.
6. Michio envisioned the final conflict between humans and artificial intelligence as natural humans vs. bionic humans. He did not foresee A.I. (artificial intelligence) or disembodied computers taking over the planet. Curiously, in Samuel Butler's nineteenth century utopian novel *Erewhon*, after which Michio and Aveline named their original natural foods store in Boston, the citizenry of this indigenous South Seas society based on natural law and healthy foods outlaw machines before they can reproduce and displace humanity. More about *Erewhon* in the *Spiral of History* volume on the industrial revolution.
7. See my recent book on the Homeric epics, *The Circle of the Dance: Achilles' Shield, Odysseus's Oar, Calypso's Axe, and the New Golden Age* (Amber Waves, 2018) for an extensive discussion of the Ages in Greek mythology.
8. Henry David Thoreau, *Walden*, 1854.
9. Plant-based diets are spreading rapidly today and have contributed to reduced rates of heart disease, many types of cancer, and other chronic diseases. But diabetes, asthma, and leukemia are on the rise among vegetarians, so for those who give up animal food, it is important to observe a well-balanced diet and lifestyle. The arc of the Spiral of History bends toward a plant-rich regimen but is not strictly vegetarian or vegan. Humanity's traditional diet included small, occasional amounts of fish, eggs, milk, or other animal-quality food. The ratio of plant to animal food varied from about

10 to 1 in the tropics to 5 to 1 in the cooler and colder regions in the world. In temperate regions, it averaged about 7 to 1, or about one to three modest servings per week. Observing these guidelines, as embodied in the contemporary macrobiotic diet, Mediterranean diet, Asian Heritage Diet, traditional Ayurvedic diet, and other balanced ways of eating, contributes to personal and social health, vitality, and longevity. Exceeding these parameters, for example, eating beef daily (altering the ratio to 4 to 1, 3 to 1, or even 2 to 1), creates imbalance at many levels—physical, psychological, intellectual, territorial, demographic, cultural, political, economic, and spiritual—as further volumes in this book will show. A strong ecological case today can be made that fish and seafood—the animal food furtherest from human beings on the evolutionary spiral and the animal quality food with the least negative and, in some cases, most beneficial impact on human health—increases toxicity and are also unsustainable. Hence, it is ideal to avoid or minimize them as much as possible until the harmony of the ocean, earth, and sky has been restored. Similarly, a plant-based diet can also lead to imbalance (e.g., organic soybean monocultures in Brazil that encroach on the rain forests). In today's world, there is plenty of grain, beans, fruits, vegetables, and other plant foods to feed everyone healthfully and affordably. Animal food, on the other hand, utilizes 10 to 25 times more energy to produce than plant foods, negatively impacts the environment and human health, and drives up the cost of farmland and the price of staples, further miring people in a downward spiral of destitution and disease Currently, 35% of all the grain now grown on the planet goes to feed animals. In the U.S. the percentage stands at 70%.

10. According to astronomers, Polaris, the current North Star, will reach its closest declination to the celestial pole about 2100 CE and then begin to decline in the night sky. This marks the beginning of a new Precessional cycle. Errai, a bright star in the constellation of Cepheus, will become the new North Star and reach its apogee between 3000 and 4000 CE. It will be followed by several other North Stars. The coming Golden Age will dawn about six thousand years later and be signified, not by a single North Star, but by the rise of the Milky Way directly overhead, showering earth with the radiance of millions of stars. For a preview of what to expect in future eras, consult the myths behind the Greek constellations of Cassiopeia and Cepheus, or comparable stories of other cultures. While the construction of the new Golden Age may ultimately lead to an enduring era of peace and harmony, the light half of the Precessional energy cycle over the next ten thousand years can be expected to experience its share of chaos and disorder, as the myths associated with these approaching constellations suggest.

The Golden Spiral

11. "Phi the Golden Number," goldennumber.net.

12. Geoffrey West, *Scales: The Universal Laws of Life and Death in Organisms, Cities, and Companies,* Weidenfeld & Nicolson, 2017.

13. In mathematics, the number e represents a constant that is the base of the natural logarithm that is equal to one. It approximates 2.71828 and is defined as the limit of n as n approaches infinity. In the abstract, this is the perfect logarithmic spiral, but on our planet, it is closer to 3.0, suggesting that our planet, like the megacities in Geoffrey West's *Scales*, is wound up and scales superlineraly at about 1.10. The Spiral of History may vibrate faster or slower on other planets. In this book, we will not try to date the different orbits of the Spiral too precisely, e.g., calculating Golden Means or exact mathematical ratios between eras and ages. There are many treatises on the-

ology, numerology, and mysticism that seek to fit historical events into an eschatological or apocalyptic framework. For example, Sir Isaac Newton, the inventor of the calculus and discoverer of the universal laws of gravitation, was obsessed with occult history. Searching for omens of the future, he compiled *The Chronology of Ancient Kingdoms Amended* that combined Chaldean astrology, Greek mythology, and other ancient sources. As historians agree, the result was a Procrustean bed of dating in which events were arbitrarily forced to fit his esoteric beliefs on alchemy and biblical prophecy. Nonetheless, Newton's conclusion that the end of days would fall about 2060 is spot on with our model that we are at an historic turning point.

14. E. J. Michael Witzel, *The Origin of the World's Mythologies,* Oxford UP, 2013.

15. For further information on the Unifying Principle, see Michio Kushi and Alex Jack, *The Book of Macrobiotics* (third edition), Square One Publications, 2012.

16. "Let food be thy medicine and thy medicine be food" is a modern, widely quoted phrase attributed to Hippocrates, but not found in his actual writings. It does, however, fairly summarize his teachings. For example, the original Hippocratic Oath states: "I will apply dietetic measures to the benefit of the sick according to my ability and judgment; I will keep them from harm and injustice." See *Ancient Medicine: Selected Papers of Ludwig Edelsein*, translated by Owsei Temkin and C. Lilian Temkin (Johns Hopkins UP, 1961).

Prehistory

17. David Reich, *Who We Are and How We Got Here: Ancient DNA and the New Science of the Human Past,* Vintage Books, 2018, p. 268. Most of the material in this section on DNA and ancestral heritage is from this book. See also Carl Zimmer, "Neanderthal Genes Hint at Much Earlier Human Migration from Africa," *New York Times*, January 31, 2020 and Arun Durvasula and Sriram Sankararam, "Recovering Signals of Ghost Archaic Introgression in African Populations," *Scientific Advances*, 6(7):2020.

18. Source: S. Lopez et al., "Human Dispersal Out of Africa: A Lasting Debate," *Evolutionary Bioinformatics Online*, 2015:11(Suppl 2), pp. 57–68,

19. David W. Anthony, *The Horse, the Wheel, and Language: How Bronze Age Riders from the Eurasian Steppes Shaped the Modern World*, Princeton UP, 2010.

20. Anthropologists are increasingly using the term "gatherer-hunters" to designate foragers rather than "hunter-gatherers" since they typically consume up to seven times more plant food than animal food. For example, in a slide show on *The Hunt*, Survival International, a nonprofit working with indigenous people around the world, notes: "Most of the hunter-gatherers' diet actually comes from gathering—not hunting. This has prompted some scientists to invert the name to 'gatherer-hunters,'" says Stephen Corry. It is thought that the ratio of vegetables to meat in the Bushman's diet is nearly 6:1, and that they eat approximately 80 different plant species." survivalinternational.com, n.d. We will follow this convention except for people like the Yamnaya, the horsemen of the steppes, who ate primarily animal food and will be called "hunter-gatherers." The Yamnaya, as noted above, also grew a major portion of their food as whole grains, so mixed food patterns were typical during a wide swath of human prehistory and history.

21. R.C. Lewontin, *The Apportionment of Human Diversity. Evolutionary Biology*, 1972, pp. 381–97.

22. Reich, *op cit.*, p. 268.

23. "Diet likely changed game for some hominids 3.5 million years ago,"

ScienceDaily.com, June 13, 2013.

24. When this evolutionary news first came out, I excitedly showed it to Michio Kushi and observed that the discovery confirmed what he had been teaching for over fifty years. In his eighty-eighth and final year, Michio read it with amusement and, with a smile, drolly commented, "Actually, our ancestors first ate wild grains 10 million years ago." New archaeological discoveries may one day push back the date back two or three times and prove him true!

25. ScienceDaily.com, *op cit*.

26. Mary Soderstrom in *Road Through Time: Humanity on the Move*, U of Regina P, 2017, pp. 17-18.

27. Coby McDonald, "Blood-Guzzling Brain Key to Evolution of Human Intelligence," Diagram "Cerebral blood flow rate in relation to estimated geological age in 12 hominin species," University of Adelaide, *Popular Science*, August 31, 2016.

28. Ferran Estebaranz et al., "Buccal dental microwear analyses support greater specialization in consumption of hard foodstuffs for *Australopithecus anamensis*," *Journal of Anthropological Sciences*, 2012; 90: 1-24.

29. Richard Alleyne, "Girls Now Reaching Puberty Before Ten—A Year Sooner than 20 Years Ago," *The Daily Telegraph* (London), June 13, 2010.

30. R. Lee Lyman, "Hunting for Evidence of Paleo-Pleistocene Hominid Scavengers, *American Anthropologist,* New Series, Vol. 89, No. 3 (September 1987), pp. 710-715.

31. "Bushmen," NationalGeographic.com, January 2000.

32. Richard Wrangham, *Catching Fire: How Cooking Made Us Human*, Basic Books 2009. See also Colin Renfrew, *Prehistory: The Making of the Human Mind*, Modern Library, 2008.

33. Evan L. Maclean, "Unraveling the evolution of uniquely human cognition," *Proceedings of the National Academy of Sciences*, 113(23):201521270, June 2016

34. Mercader J., "Mozambican grass seed consumption during the Middle Stone Age," *Science*. 2009 Dec 18;326(5960):1680-3.

35. "The Stone Age baker: Cavemen 'ate bread, not just meat,'" *Daily Mail Reporter*, October 19, 2010.

36. Marcel Kornfield, "Are Paleoindians of the Great Plains and Rockies subsistence specialists?" In *Foragers of the Terminal Pleistocene in North America*, edited by Renee Walker and Boyce Driskell, U Nebraska P, 2007.

37. JoAnna Klein, "Did Dietary Changes Bring Us 'F' Words? Study Tackles Complexities of Language's Origins," *New York Times*, March 14, 2019.

38. "The Physiological Function of the Cereal Awn," *Botanical Review* 29(3):1963:366-81.

39. William Blake, "Auguries of Innocence," 1803. For a comprehensive exploration of awns, see Alex Jack, Bettina Zumdick, and Edward Esko, *Awned, the New Organic*, Amber Waves Press, 2017.

40. Rivka Elbaum et al., "The Role of Wheat Awns in the Seed Dispersal Unit," *Science* 11 May 2007, 3165826), 884-886.

41. Michio Kushi with Alex Jack, *One Peaceful World*, revised edition, Square One, 2017, pp. 83-90.

42. See "Comet May Have Exploded Over Canada 12,900 Years Ago After All, *Science News*, September 18, 2012. See also Graham Hancock, *The Magicians of the Gods*, Griffin, 2017, for a detailed summary of the scientific evidence for this comet and its impact.

43. Michio Kushi strongly believed in the existence of several lost continents and an

ancient wisdom tradition that encircled the planet about 20,000 years ago when the Milky Way was ascendant. There are tantalizing scientific hints of this era, which he called the Ancient Scientific and Spiritual World Community. This is very suggestive and appealing, but there is not enough scientific evidence to support this theory, and it is not included, nor essential, to this study of the historical spiral. For my own exploration of possible psychic and spiritual dimensions to history, see *A Visit to the Land of the Gods* (One Peaceful World Press, 1998) in which I describe visiting the leading authority on the Takeuchi Documents, ancient Japanese scrolls purportedly describing the hidden history of the world.

44. Giorgio de Santillana and Hertha von Dechend, *Hamlet's Mill*, Godine, 1981. See Alex Jack's edition of *Hamlet* by Christopher Marlowe and William Shakespeare, Amber Waves Press, 2005, for an extended commentary on this theme. *Hamlet* has numerous references and allusions to the Precessional myth and the coming New Era of Humanity.

45. Neil L. Thomas, "Stonehenge and the Fibonacci Code," n.d., megalithic.co.uk.

Five Peaceful Civilizations

46. Homer, *The Odyssey*, translated by Robert Fitzgerald, Doubleday, 1961. All quotations from the *Odyssey* in this section are from this translation.

47. See Gavin Menzies, *The Lost Empire of Atlantis*, William Morrow, 2011, for compelling evidence that the Minoans sailed to North America and had a trade outpost on Lake Superior where they brought copper from mines back to Europe via the Mississippi River, Gulf Coast, and Atlantic Ocean.

48. There is archaeological evidence at three late Minoan sites of human sacrifice, but these all occurred on Crete after the Thera volcanic explosion and may represent elements of Mycenean culture.

49. For a comprehensive discussion of Odysseus's quest to balance female energy, including material from mythologist Joseph Campbell, see Alex Jack, "Calypso's Butterfly Axe," *The Circle of the Dance*, Amber Waves Press, 2018, pp. 154-175. Because of the strong suppression of women throughout most of the Spiral of History, many women have written under male pseudonyms. Some of the world's greatest literature not only has a feminist orientation, but also may have been composed by a female. English novelist Samuel Butler contended that the *Odyssey* was written by a woman—Nausicaa, the princess who rescued Odysseus when he washed ashore. Critic Harold Bloom argued that the J source in the Hebrew Bible was a woman, and intriguing cases have been advanced that Mary Sidney (a Protestant poet) or Amelia Bassano Lanier (a poet of Jewish heritage) wrote the Shakespearean canon. For the case for Amelia, see Alex Jack, editor, *As You Like It* by Christopher Marlowe and William Shakespeare, Amber Waves, 2012, pp. 227-239.

50. With their inferior gymnastic skills, Athenian athletes who participated in this proto-Aegean Olympiad may have been injured, or even killed, in the dangerous competition. In Athens, their sacrifice could have given rise to the Minos story.

51. For a fascinating account of the Minoans and an intriguing deciphering of the Phaistos Disk, see Alan Butler, *The Dawn of Genius*, Watkins, 2014.

52. Quoted in Robert Graves, *The White Goddess*, FSG (second edition), 2014. Graves says the labyrinth was probably the site of a ritual performance in honor of the Moon Goddess.

53. "The Legacy of Ban Chiang," Royal Thai Embassy, Washington, D.C. thaiembdc.org, April 20, 2016.

54. Roderick J. McIntosh, *Ancient Middle Niger: Urbanism and the Self-Organizing Landscape,* Cambridge UP, 2005.

55. Ibid, 137. *See also* McIntosh*, The Peoples of the Middle Niger,* Blackwell, 1988.

56. Captain James Cook, *Logbook,* 1770.

57. As in many cultures, Aboriginal myths and stories include tales of elopement, violence, abduction, and rape. Both men and women who violated initiation rites, incest taboos, and other sacred practices could be punished (e.g., spearing in the thigh) or condemned to death (by stones, sharpened bones, or sorcery). In respect to domestic violence, ancient Aboriginal female skeletons display a much higher degree of skull and other bone fractures than those of males. Stephen Webb, *Palaeo-pathology of Aboriginal Australians*. Cambridge UP, 1995, p. 2.

58. Quoted in Bill Gummage, *The Biggest Estate on Earth: How the Aboriginals Made Australia*, Allen & Unwin, 2013.

59. Ibid., passim.

60. Joel J. Schaefer, *Serving People with Food Allergies: Kitchen Management and Menu Creation*, CRC Press, 2011, p. 97.

61. Gummage, *op cit.*, p. 185.

62. Native people in the American desert Southwest have similar traditions. Asked why they settled in the most inhospitable regions, when more pleasant environs were available, they replied that they chose to do so to show their faith in the creator's bounty and protection.

63. See Gary Holz, D.Sc. and Robbie Holz, *Secrets of Aboriginal Healing*, Bear & Co., 2013, for the story of an American scientist who had a crippling condition and went to live with an indigenous community in the outback that could communicate telepathically. Telepathy reportedly continues to exist among the Tabu, ethnic herders and nomads in parts of Chad, Libya, Niger, and Sudan; Maoris in New Zealand; and other indigenous people.

64. Webb, *op cit*, p. 293.

65. P.A.S. Wurm et al., "Australian Native Rice: A new sustainable wild food enterprise," Rural Industries Research and Development Corporation, 2011.

66. This traditional Australian folktale on the compassion of animals is strikingly similar to the *Jataka Tales* in Buddhism. These pithy stories relate the previous births of Gautama Buddha (often in animal form), in which he perfects some virtue.

67. Gerda Lerner, *The Creation of Patriarchy*, Oxford UP, 1987, p. 39.

68. For an in-depth survey of ancient Dogon wisdom, see the series of books on comparative cosmology by Laird Scranton, including *The Science of the Dogon*, Inner Traditions, 2002, and *Sacred Symbols of the Dogon*, Inner Traditions, 2007.

Codas

69. There have been virtually no scientific studies on how food is cooked and its impact on health and well-being. Anecdotally, macrobiotic dietary counselors, including myself and many colleagues, consistently observe that when cancer patients or those with other serious ills change from electrical and microwave cooking to gas their likelihood of improvement and recovery significantly increases.

70. Examples of flawed ideologies and mass delusional thinking today include the Republican senators who acquitted President Trump in the Impeachment Trial, the Catholic Church's long denial and subsequent coverup of widespread sexual molestation by priests, and the opioid crisis fueled by the pharmaceutical industry and modern medicine, as well as authoritarian governments around the world.

Index

Ableism, 39
Aboriginal Australia, 8, 83, 104-113, 115, 133
Accelerating pace of life, 30, 34
Adriane, 89, 91
Advance by Idea, 31, 42, 71
Afghanistan, 86, 94
Africa, 50, 52, 62, 78, 97. *See also Niger River Valley Civilization*.
African Americans, 17
Age of Discovery, 50
Age of Ideology, 29
Age of Steel, 39
Age of Sustainability, 29
Ageism, 39
Ages of Humanity, 9, 20-21, 37-38
Aging, 40
Agricultural Revolution, 22, 26, 37, 117
Agriculture, 59, 77, 78, 95; god of, 8. *See Tjiwara*.
AI, 27, 34, 128
AIDS, 35, 119
Airplane, 8
Ainu, 61
Akrotiri, 89, 91
Alcinous, 84, 85
Alcohol, 41
Algorithms, 17, 34
Alpaca, 113-114
Altair, 79
Amazon (company), 34, 49
Amazon River, 51, 59, 62, 78, 102
Amur River basin, 61
Anatolia, 97
Ancient World, 20, 29, 33, 49, 90, 94, 117
Andaman Islands, 51, 62
Andes, 102, 115
Animal food, in Australian diet, 105, 108, 110; and increased consumption following the Out of Africa migration 50, 51; increased intake during Bronze Age 38; and Iron Age, 39; and climate change, 40, 129; in Lurasian mythology, 10; in the *Odyssey*, 85; increased consumption and onset of menarche, 66; 7:1 ratio to plant food, 53; standard amount in traditional diets, 54, 55, 128-129, 130; and structure of teeth 28; in tropics, 53, 128-129
Animal messengers, 114, 124
Antelope, 93, 99, 112, 113, 114, 123
Ants, 106
Apes, 63, 64
Apple, 49
Aquarian Age, 21, 72

Arete, 85
Arlington Street Church, 22
Armenia, 60
Armies, 92
Artificial Reproductive Technologies 27, 34, 36, 72, 120
Art, 98-99, 104, 115
Ashoka, 51
Assyria, 87
Astrological Ages, 72
Athena, 85
Athens, 91, 132
Atlantis, 78, 81
Atomic Age, 29
Australapithecus anamensis, 65
Australians, 51, 59, 70, 93
Australopithecus robustus, 68
Australopithicines, 64
Australopithicus afarensis, 68
Austria, 58
Austroasians, 62
Awns, 8, 9, 38, 115, 131; in African rice, 96; and ancestral food, 52; as antennae, 75; and "bearded" wheat, 73, 74; definition of, 9; and earth's energy, 75-76; and higher consciousness, 75-76; in rice, 112; use among Five Peaceful Civilizations, 113
Axis shift, 65, 77
Ayurvedic diet, 129
Aztec, 21, 38, 51

Babylon, 87
Back to Africa, 58
Bambara, 99
Ban Chiang, 94
Bantu, 62
Barley, 9, 38, 39, 53, 60, 75, 76, 85, 86, 88, 94, 113
Basal Europeans, 59
Beads, 93, 97
Beans, 37, 53, 54, 78, 102, 129
Bearded wheat, 74, 75
Bears, 122
Beatniks, 53
Bee, 119, 122
Beef, 39, 129
Beethoven, 44, 52
Bell Beaker Culture, 60
Beloved (Morrison), 52
Bemba, 100
Benin, 95
Berber, 98
Bering Strait, 61

Index

Bible 52, 77, 132
Big Dipper, 79
Biological evolution, 47, 48, 63-67, 123
Bionics, 120
Bionization, 36
Birds, 122
Black Death, 26, 35, 52
Black Sea, 59, 70, 86
Blacksmiths, 100-101
Blake, William, 75
Bloom, Harold, 132
Bodhisattva, 8
Bonobos, 67, 68, 122-123
Borobudur, 43
Bow and arrow, 77
Brain size, 64
Brave New World (Huxley), 36
Brillat-Savarin, Jean Athelme, 37
British Isles, 59, 60
Bronze Age, 20, 38, 60, 78, 86
Brown rice, 11, 38, 53, 113
Buckwheat, 53
Buddha, 22, 31, 51, 133
Buddhism, 17, 22, 51, 133
Bull, 79, 80, 89, 90, 91, 93, 113
Bulletin of the Atomic Scientists, 20
Bush Tucker, 110
Bushmen, 66, 130
Butler, Samuel, 128, 132
Byamee, 109, 112, 115

Caesarean Section, 36
Calypso, 88
Campbell, Joseph, 132
Campfire, 71, 119
Cancer, 35, 36
Capital punishment, 111, 133
Capitalism, 39
Caral, 101, 102, 116
Caspian Sea, 59
Cassiopeia, 129
Cat, 78
Catholic Church, 133
Cattle, 39, 40, 60, 77, 78, 94, 125
Celestial navigation, 116
Cell phones, 27
Celtics, 80
Central Africa, 59, 62, 62, 71, 98
Central America, 102
Central Asia, 51, 59
Centripetal and centrifugal, 11, 16, 30, 47, 54, 118
Cepheus, 129
Cereal grains, 52-53
Chaco Canyon, 79
Chad, 133
Chakra, 9, 34, 46, 74
Charcoal, 16, 70, 119
Chartres, 43
Chauvet cave, 81
Chemical farming, 24, 39, 40, 119
Chemicals, 63, 119
Chichen Itza, 8
Chicken, 39, 78
Children, 18, 39, 52, 65, 83, 99, 112, 114

Chimpanzees, 63, 64, 67, 68, 122
China, 8, 24, 38, 44, 61, 77, 78, 92, 112, 116, 120
Chinese medicine, 45
Christianity, 17, 51
Cities, in Crete, 86; rise of city-states, 11, 26, 30, 41, 78, 83; built without fortifications, 74, 87, 94, 103; in the Indus Valley, 91, 93, 94; in South America, 102, 129; and spiral dynamics, 11, 48, 49, 129; in West Africa, 95, 96, 97; oldest, 59
Civilization, 9, 115, 116, 120
Classless societies, 97, 105, 111, 114
Clay, 51, 94, 98, 105
Climate change, and Aboriginal solutions, 108, and the Age of Sustainability, 29; and destruction by fire, 119; and the digital revolution, 27; and geo-engineering, 40; and the modern food system, 36; and plant-based foods, 41; and the Spiral of History, 1,16, 17, 39; visualization to mitigate, 126; and world federal government, 120
Cline, 9
Clothing, 71, 103, 104
Clovis, 71
Cold War, 15, 20
Columbian Exchange, 38
Comet, 76-77, 119
Computer, 8, 28, 29, 32, 33, 34, 39, 40,
Computer Age, 29, 42, 50, 125
Condiments, 38, 53
Confucianism, 51
Confucius, 51
Cook, James, 104, 106
Cooking, 55; in ancient Europe, 70; and human evolution, 63-67; impact on health, 133-134; discovery of 64, 66, 71; use of hot rocks for, 102 104: misuse of, 119; proto-cooking by animals, 122; and spiral measurements, 44, 55
Copper, 72, 86, 93, 96, 97, 114, 132
Copper Age, 50, 60, 78
Corded Ware Culture, 60
Coronavirus, 1, 119
Cotton, 94, 96, 102
Creation of Adam, The (Michelangelo), 8, 44
Crete, 59, 86, 89, 115
Crows, 122
Cubism, 52, 101
Cyberhacking, 40
Cyclops, 90

Dairy, 53
Dance, 55, 72, 91, 99, 106
Dancing Girl of Mohenjo-Daro, 92-93
Dante, 8, 52, 121
Dark matter, 27
Date palms, 95
Dawkins, Richard, 20
De Santillana, Giorgio, 79
Deneb, 79
Denisovans, 57, 58, 64, 68
Dentistry, 94
Diet, of animals, 63-64, 122-124; Australian, 108; of early hominids, 68-69; of the Five Peaceful Civilizations, 115; guidelines for, 40; in the *Odyssey*, 85; and the ratio of plant to animal food, 128-129; and speech, 71; of traditional

human, 11; and world history 37-38
Dietary Goals for the United States, 35, 36, 39, 128
Digital revolution, 27, 33, 37, 39, 117
Digital surveillance, 40
Dingo, 104, 111
Dinkinesh (Lucy), 50, 65
Disabled, 40
Divine Comedy (Dante), 8, 52, 121
Djenne Djeno, 96, 97, 98
DNA, 47-48; of Africans, 62; of Andeans, 59; of Denisovans in Australia, 104; and human evolution, 57-63; of humans mixed with Neanderthals and Denisovans, 59; shared between humans and other primates, 67; of Iberian males, 61; of South Indians, 61; and Star Clusters, 60-61
Doctor Zhivago (Pasternak), 52
Dog, 77, 78, 122
Dogon, 116, 133
Dolmens, 78
Dolni Vestonice, 70
Dolphins, 110
Double axe, 88
Draco, 78
Dreamtime, 105, 109, 111, 112
Dravidian, 93

e, 129
Eagle, 78
East Africa, 59, 62, 65, 68, 97
East Asia, 51, 53, 57, 58, 59, 61, 117
Ebola, 35, 119
Egypt, 8, 24, 38, 59, 78, 79 87, 92, 94, 114, 116; culture of, 100; hieroglyphs, 98; mythology of, 99
Einstein, Albert, 8
Electrical cooking, 119, 133-134
Elephant, 93, 123
Electromagnetic energy, 78; fields, 27, 119
Empedocles, 91
Emu Dreaming, 109
Energy consumption, 16, 26, 34
England, 80, 104
Environmental crisis, 38
Epidemics, 26, 35, 39, 41, 119, 125
Epigenetics, 9
Epoch, 42
Equinox, 11, 41, 42, 72, 73, 79, 81, 118, 120
Erectus, Homo, 57, 58, 64, 65, 66, 68, 71
Erewhon (Samuel Butler), 128
Errai, 129
Eskimo-Aleut languages, 61
Ethiopia, 62
Europe, 10, 15, 18, 51, 53, 58-61, 69, 70, 77, 80, 83, 86, 90, 91, 97, 104, 106, 107, 132
Evans, Sir Arthur, 87
Evolution, animal, 112, 113, 129; biological, 1, 17, 21, 22, 25, 36, 47, 48, 52; and cooking, 63-67, 123; cosmic, 22, 47; human, 10, 17, 57, 64-67, 70-72, 123, 131; human embryo, 48; reverse, 36; spiritual, 1, 17, 36 , 113
F sound, 70
Facebook, 49
Farming, 4, 105, 113, 119, 120, 124, 125, 131. *See also Agriculture*.
Faro, 100, 115

Fasting, 56
Female egalitarianism, 115; energy, 31, 132; domination, 26, 66-67; egalitarianism, 115; and earth and sky, 99. *See Women*. .
Feminism, 111, 115
Fertile Crescent, 18, 51, 117
Fibonacci series, 45, 46, 80
Fire, 16; in Australia, 105-108; in cooking, 64; and culture-bearers, 73; destruction by, 119; discovery of, 71, 123; and human evolution, 47; put out by elephants and rhinos, 123; uses of, 66; uses of by bonobos, 122-123, by birds of prey, 123
Firehawk, 123
Fish and seafood, 53, 65, 97, 110, 113, 122, 129
Fishing, 96, 102, 110
Five Peaceable Civilizations, 9-10, 18, 38, 51, 83-117; commonalities among, 113-117
Floods, 77
Flores islanders, 58
Floresiensis, Homo, 68
Flute, 8, 15, 52, 72, 102
Food Guide Pyramid, 35, 36, 40
Foraging, 29, 114
Fractal, 10, 16
France, 15, 79, 81
Freudian, 30
Fruit, 11, 28, 39, 41, 53, 63, 64, 65, 67, 70, 71, 74, 78, 94, 102, 110, 114, 129
Fruitarian, 63

Galactic Year, 47
Galapagos, 122
Gandhi, Mohandas, 17, 51
Gatherer-Hunters, 10, 79, 100, 130
Gaugin, Paul, 18
Gazelle, 94, 113, 114, 123
Gender, 26, 113, 114
Gene-edited foods, 41
Genesis, 81
Genetic engineering, 20, 27, 29, 35, 40, 119-121
Genocide, 26, 27, 38
Geoengineering, 40, 120
Georgia, 66
Germany, 8, 59, 72
Ghana, 95
Ghost Modern, 62
Ghost population, 59, 61, 62, 82
Gilgamesh, Epic of, 8, 52, 77
Global warming, 17, 27, 35, 36, 39, 55, 78, 108, 119, 120, 121, 126
GMOs, 27, 39, 41
Goats, 77, 78, 94
Gobekli Tepe, 79
Golden Age, 20, 37-38, 72-75; end of, 81; and the Minoans, 90; new, 41, 129; and Ovid's description of, 73, 74; and Phaeacia, 86; and Vega, 78
Golden Apples of the Hesperides, 78
Golden Diet, 52-56
Golden Mean, 49, 90, 129-130
Golden Ratio, 10, 44-45; and diet, 52-56; and Chauvet cave; and Stonehenge, 80
Golden Rectangle, 44-45
Golden Spiral, 43-56
Gondwanan mythology, 10, 51, 99, 112

Index

Google, 49
Gorbachev, Mikhail, 51-52
Gorilla, 68
Grain, animal vs. human use of, 129; animal consumption of, 123; and ancient food processing of, 68, 70-71; coevolution with humans, 63-64; and evolution, 47
Gravettian culture, 59
Great Goddess, 115
Great Lakes (Africa), 50, 96
Great Mosque of Kairouan, 43
Great Pyramid, 8, 43, 44, 78
Great Year, 41-42, 72, 73
Greece, 51, 59, 94, 116, 117; mythology of, 37; philosophy of, 30
Green technology, 17
Greenhouse gases, 34
Gregorian chant, 52
Groundnuts, 95
Guanyin, 8
Guava, 102
Guinea, 95
Guinea fowl, 96
Gujarat, 93
Gummage, Bill, 108

Habilis, Homo, 64, 65, 68, 71
Hakra Ware, 93
Hamburger, 8
Hamlet (Marlowe and Shakespeare), 79
Harai, Yuval Noah, 16
Harappa, 91, 94, 113, 116
Hawk, 46
Heart disease, 36, 41
Hegelian, 30
Hegsted, Mark, 128
Hephaestus, 38
Heracles, 78
Hesiod, 38
Hildegard of Bingen, 8, 51
Hinduism, 8, 17, 22, 30, 37, 51
Hipparchus, 72
Hippocrates, 53-54, 130
Holocene, 77
Holy Grail, 52
Homer, 38, 52, 84
Hominid, 10, 63, 68-69
Hominin, 10, 25, 28, 58, 64, 67, 68, 104, 114, 123
Homo, 10
Homophobia, 39
Hopi, 21
Horse, 77, 78, 116
Hot rocks, 103, 119, 122
Human, early diet, 64-67; form, 45, 48; origin and destiny, 50-52; sacrifice, 132
Humus, 53
Hungary, 80
Hunter-gatherers, 66
Hunting, 51, 64, 66, 67, 71, 77, 94, 104, 114, 130
Huxley, Aldous, 36
Hyoid, 71

Iberia, 60, 61
Ice age, 66

Iguanas, 122
Iliad (Homer), 38, 52
Implant, 120
Impressionism, 52
India, 8, 61, 66, 78, 91; medicine of, 45
Indigenous people, 9, 26, 39, 40, 51, 61, 62, 70, 105, 109, 111, 128, 130, 133
Indo-Aryans, 60
Indonesia, 58, 66
Induction cooking, 119
Indus Sarvasati Civilization, 78, 91-94, 114; absence of war in, 94; cooking in, 94; culture of, 115; diet of, 94; farming in, 59; script of, 93; and trade with the Minoans, 86
Industrial Revolution, 26, 33, 37, 117
Industrialization, 119
Inequality, 61
Inka, 8, 38, 51, 59, 103, 116
Insects, 45, 48, 65, 67, 69, 108, 110, 119, 122
iPhone, 8
Iran, 60, 61
Iron, 96
Iron Age, 38, 39
Irradiated food, 39
Isaiah, 51
Islam, 51, 99, 116
Israel, ancient, 8, 116
Italy, 69
Ivory Coast, 95

Jack, Homer A., 20
Jan Breughel the Elder, 84
Japan, 61, 112
Jataka Tales, 133
Jericho, 59
Jesus, 8, 22, 51
Jewelry, 71, 86, 92-94, 98, 100, 114,
Journey to the West (Wu-Chen En), 52
Joyce, James, 17
Judaism, 51

Kalahari bushmen, 66
Kali Yuga, 20, 39
Kandahar, 94
Kangaroo, 110, 111-113, 114
Keftiu, 87
Kerosene, 119
King, Martin Luther, Jr., 8, 17, 41, 51
Knossos, 86, 87, 89, 90
Kokopelli, 8
Kola nuts, 95, 99
Korean War, 39
Krishna, 8
Kukulcan Pyramid, 81
Kushi, Aveline, 53, 54
Kushi, Michio; 5, 8, 22, 53, 54; and the health revolution, 35-36; and medical research, 128; on human origins, 131; on lost continents, 132; predictions by, 128; and the original Spiral of History, 24; prayers, meditations, and visualizations, 124; and spiral teachings, 47; and the Unifying Principle, 52

Labrys, 88-89

Labyrinth, 89
LaDuke, Winona, 14
Lake Chad, 96
Landbridge, 61
Language, 61, 71, 123
Lanier, Amelia Bassano, 132
Laozi, 31, 40, 51
Lascaux, 79
Last Supper, The (Leonardo) 44
LBGTQ, 40
Lee, Ann, 51
Lemuria, 78
Leonardo da Vinci, 8, 44
Lerner, Gerda, 114
Les Demoiselles d'Avignon (Picasso), 101
Lewontin, R.C. 63
Linear A, 91
Literature, 132
Llama, 113, 114
Logarithmic spiral, 10-11, 43, 44-46, 129-130
Lotus root, 110
Louvre, 98
Lunar cycles, 79
Lurasian mythology, 10, 51, 112

Ma'at, 8
Macrobiotics, 53, 54, 129
Mahabharata, 52
Maize, 39, 53, 102, 113
Mali, 8, 97, 100, 116
Malnutrition, 39
Mammoth, 70
Mandé, 95, 100, 101
Mandela, Nelson, 52
Maori, 133
Marlowe, Christopher, 8
Marsupial, 111
Marxism-Leninism, 30, 51
Mary (Virgin), 51
Masculine energy, 31, 99
Matrilineal, 90, 114
Maya, 8, 21, 38, 51, 81, 116
McGovern, George, 35
McIntosh, Roderick, 97, 100, 101
Meat, use among primates, 67; in the traditional human diet, 53, 65
Medicine Lodge Creek, 70
Medieval Age, 29, 33
Mediterranean diet, 129
Megalith, 78
Mehrgarh, 93-94
Melanesia, 51
Menarche, 65-66
Mental and emotional health, 28, 40
Mesoamerica, 9, 21, 59, 77
Mesopotamia, 29, 60, 86, 92, 93, 96, 114
Message stick, 109, 115
Metallurgy, 71, 100, 105, 106, 114, 123
Mexico, 29, 30, 81
Michelangelo, 8, 44
Microbiome, 28
Microchip implants, 36
Microwave, 119, 133-134
Middle Stone Age, 76

Militarism, 26, 114, 116
Milky Way, 72, 73, 76, 109, 121, 129, 132
Millet, 44, 5 3, 61, 70, 96, 110, 113; and kangaroos, 112; and Nok art, 98-99; and Tjiwara, 99
Mindfulness, 120
Minoan 84-91; absence of war, 87-88; art, 90, 113; collapse, 89; culture, 115; diet and peacefulness of, 91; and Golden Age, 90; and Golden Mean, 90; matrilineal social structure, 114-115; and possible contact with North America, 132; women's role, 87
Minos, King, 86-87, 89, 90, 132
Minotaur, 89
Modern Age, 29, 33
Mohenjo-Daro, 91, 92, 116
Mollusks, 122
Mona Lisa (Leonardo), 8, 44
Monarchy, 26, 92, 97, 100, 114, 116
Moon race, 8, 15, 34
Morocco, 57-58
Moravia, 69
Morrison, Toni, 52
Moses, 8, 51
Mother Goddess, 113
Mozambique, 68
Mozart, 44, 52
Muhammad, 8, 51
Music, 52, 72, 104; and agriculture, 55; Australian instruments, 105; and quipu, 102; oldest instrument, 72
Mycenaean, 61, 86, 89

Na Dene, 61
Nabta Playa, 79-80
Native Americans 8, 15,21, 59, 61-62, 133
Natural gas, 119-120
Natural sweeteners, 53
Nautilus, 15
Neanderthals, Homo, 57, 64, 68; and African ancestry, 62; breeding with Sapiens, 59; and Denisovan common ancestor, 58
Needham, Joseph, 22
Neolithic, 20, 57, 60, 76, 80, 86, 94, 100, 115
Neuron, 10, 28, 35, 36
New Era of Humanity, 42, 117, 118-121
New Grange, 80, 81
New Guinea, 59, 62, 104
New Zealand, 104
Newton, Isaac, 30, 130
Ngalue, 68
Niger River Valley Civilization, 38, 83, 95-101, 113-115
Noah, 77
Nok, 98
Nomads, 79
Norte Chico Civilization, 10, 18, 38, 101-104, 113, 114, 116
North America, 10, 51, 53, 55, 59, 61, 62, 70, 77, 78, 83, 120, 132, 133
North Star, 72-73, 118, 119, 121, 129
Notre Dame, 43
Nubia, 79
Nuclear energy, 8, 40, 120; threat, 20, 21, 30; war, 27, 119; waste, 40; weapons,120

Index

Nutcracker Man, 65
Nuts, 11, 37, 53, 63, 64, 66, 70, 71, 94, 95, 99, 110, 122, 123
Nyama, 100

Oats, 53
Oceania, 61
Odysseus, 84-89, 90, 132
Odyssey (Homer), 38, 52, 84-89, 90, 91, 132
Ohsawa, George, 22, 52
Old Europe, 80
Old Stone Age, 76
Oman, 93
Opioid crisis, 134
Orangutans, 68
Orion, 80
Osiris, 91
Out of Africa, 50-51, 57-59, 62, 66
Ovid, 73, 74
Pakistan, 59, 78, 91, 94

Paleolithic era, 20, 25, 57, 58, 69, 70, 72, 76, 79, 100, 119
Pan-Gaean mythology, 50-51
Papua New Guinea, 70
Paradise, 76
Paris, 98
Parker, Theodore, 17
Parks, Rosa, 51
Parrots, 122
Parthenon, 43, 44, 91
Parzival (von Echenbach), 8, 52
Patriarchy, 10, 60, 61, 112, 117
Patrilineal descent, 104-105
Peace movement, 53
Pearl millet, 98
Peas, 95
Penelope, 86
Persia, 59
Peru, 101, 114, 115
Petroglyph, 15
Phaeacia, 84-89, 90
Phaistos Disk, 91, 132
Pharmaceuticals, 119, 134
Pharaoh, 100
Picasso, Pablo, 101
Pigs, 77, 78, 94
Plant vs. animal food, 38-39, 116, 128-129, 130
Plastics, 119
Plato, 51, 72, 81
Platonic Year, 72
Plumbing, 86, 115
Pneuma, 100
Polaris, 41, 76, 118, 119, 121, 129
Polynesians, 104
Pork, 39
Poseidon, 90
Pontic-Caspian Steppe, 60
Pottery, 8, 93, 94, 97, 98, 102, 116, 124
Precession of the Equinoxes, 11, 41, 42, 72-73, 118, 119, 121, 129
Pre-Columbian America, 18
Pregnancy, 65-66
Prehistory, 29, 57-82

Prejudice and discrimination, 41
Priesthood, 26, 92, 93
Principal food, 70-71
Proto-Indo European, 60
Proto-Saharan, 97, 98
Psychedelic movement, 53
Psychonization, 36
Pyramid, 8, 11, 102, 101, 102, 113
Qi, 11, 100, 119
Quinoa, 53, 102, 113
Quipu, 102

Rabia, 51
Radioactivity, 40
Rainbow Serpent, 8, 109
Raw food, 66
Reel, Jeffrey, 40
Refined grain, 41
Reich, David, 16, 57, 63
Religion 83, 93, 100, 115-116
Renaissance, 6, 8, 29, 30, 38, 42, 43, 49, 50, 52
Rhinoceros, 81, 123
Rice, 53, 70, 110; in Africa, 95, 96; Asian vs. Australian, 112; farming in China, 61; eaten by kangaroos, 112
Rice Coast, 95
Rift Valley, 50
Robot, 27, 29, 34, 39
Rock art, 15, 98, 104
Romania, 80
Rome, 51, 97, 116, 117; mythology of, 37; pottery of, 94
Rule by Power, 31, 42, 71
Russia, 60, 69
Rye, 53, 75

Sahara, 95, 98, 114
Salt, 97
San, 66
Sanskrit, 61
Santorini, 89, 91
Sapiens, Homo, 57-59, 62, 64, 68
Sapolsky, Robert, 16
Sarvasati, goddess, 13; river, 116
Saturn, 45, 46
Savanna, 100
Scale: The Universal Laws of Growth, Innovation, Sustainability, and the Pace of Life (West), 48-49
Scandinavia, 59, 79
Scheria, 84-86
School shootings, 38
Sea-Reach 84, 88
Seasonings, 53
Sedentism, 79
Sedges, 11, 64, 65, 71
Seeds, 11, 37, 53, 63, 64, 65, 70, 71, 75, 76, 94, 99, 100, 107, 109, 110, 114
Seven Ages, 29
7:1 ratio, 27-29, 47, 51, 54, 55, 63, 129
Sexual emancipation, 26
Sexual equality, 113, 114
Shakespeare, 44, 132
Sheep, 77, 78, 94
Shell, 26, 27, 71, 93, 102, 109, 110, 122

Shelley, Percy and Mary, 52
Siberia, 51, 59, 60, 61-62
Sidney, Mary, 132
Sierra Leone, 95
Silk, 78
Silver Age, 13, 20, 38, 81
Sino-Tibetan language, 61
Sirius, 80, 116
Sixties, 53
Slavery 26, 39, 97, 111, 116
Smallpox, 52
Smartphone, 39
Smelting, 96, 114
Smithsonian Institution, 22
Social Gospel, 17
Socrates, 51
Soderstrom, Mary, 64
Solstice, 79, 80
Somalia, 62
Songlines, 108-109
Songs, Australian, 106
Sorghum, 53, 68, 70, 79, 96
South Africa, 71
South America, 10, 18, 51, 53, 59, 62, 78, 83, 101, 102, 103, 113, 114
South Asia, 93, 117
Southeast Asia, 61, 93, 104
Southern Cross, 109
Spaceship, 25
Spain, 86
Spices, 94
Spiral, in the ancient world, 15, 43; of biological evolution, 52; center of, 33-34; in cities, 49; in companies, 49; of consciousness, 28-29; and cookware, 44; of the cosmos, 47; of creation, 47; of elements and particles, 47; of the equinoxes, 118-119; and exponential rates of change, 49; golden, 43-56; of the Golden Diet, 54; of the human form 28, 45, 48; of human culture, 71-72; of human embryo, 48; of human evolution, 70-72; of legs, 28; of life and creation, 27; logarithmic, 43; at New Grange, 80; and nutrients, 28, 54; of plant and animal life, 48; sevenfold, 27-28; of the solar system, 47; of the teeth, 28
Spiral of History, 11, 20-42; yang view, 23; yin view, 23
Sponheimer, Matt, 63-64
Squash, 102
Staff God, 102
Star Clusters, 60
Stateless societies, 104, 114
Steel, 96
Steppes, 59
Stone, for architecture, 79, 103; for art, 58; circles, 78-80; for cooking and cookware, 55, 70, 102, 104, 105; for energy generation, 109; for engraving, 91; for building, 59; precious and semi-precious, 93, 109; ship turned to, 85, 90; standing, 78, 80, 82, 101, 103; for stoning to death, 123; for tools, 65, 68, 71, 105, 111, 122, 123
Stone Age, 70, 76
Stonehenge, 8, 80-81
Storytelling, 104
Sugar, 41

Sumer, 4, 38, 77, 78, 87, 92, 94, 116
Sun Dagger, 79
Sundiata, 52, 97, 101
Survival International, 130
Sustainability, 40, 111, 116, 120
Swedenberg, 22
Sweet potatoes, 102, 122
Sydney, 105
Syria, 59, 86

Tabu, 133
Tagore, 51
Taiqi, 120
Taj Mahal, 8, 43, 44
Takeuchi Documents, 132
Teeth, 28, 65, 70, 123
Telepathy, 109, 133
Tempeh, 53
Ten Commandments, 8
Thailand, 94
Thera, 89, 90
Theseus, 89
Thomas, Neil L., 80
Thoreau, Henry David, 40
Thuban, 78
Thunberg, Greta, 8
Tibet, 61
Tifinagh, 98
Tiger, 93
Timaeus (Plato), 72
Timbuktu, 95, 98
Tiresias, 85
Tjiwara, 8, 11, 101, 114, 124, 99-100
Tofu, 53
Tools, 8, 47, 65, 66, 68, 71-72, 81, 88, 105, 111, 114, 124
Torres Strait, 104, 105
Totora, 102
Toynbee, Arnold, 22, 31-32
Toys, 94
Trade, 85, 86, 91, 92, 97, 102, 109, 111, 114, 132
Transportation, 34, 104, 120
Tree of Life, 8
Trireme, 8
Trojan War, 38, 84-85
Troy, 94
Trump, Donald, 133
Truth, Sojourner, 8
Turkey, 59
Twain, Mark, 14, 15

Ukraine, 60
Ultra-processed food, 39, 41
Unifying Principle 52
Unitarianism, 22
University of Colorado, Boulder, 63
Unrecorded history, 76
Upanishads, 14, 37
Ussher, Bishop, 50

Vedic India, 8, 20, 38, 92, 112, 116
Vega, 76, 78, 79
Vegan, 39

Index

Vegetables, 28, 37, 39, 41, 53, 54, 63, 71, 78, 125, 129, 130
Vegetarians, 128
Venus, 45
Venus of Willendorf, 8, 58
Vicuna, 101, 113, 114
Vietnam War, 39
Violence, 66, 112, 116, 133; absence of, 94, 97, 115
Virachoca, 102
Volcano, 89, 115
Waal, Frans de, 67
Walden (Thoreau), 40
War, 15, 17, 18, 26, 27, 29, 31, 33, 37, 38, 39, 40, 51, 112; absence of, 10, 18, 94, 102, 105, 111, 115. *See also Civil War, Cold War, Cyberwar, Nuclear War, World War I, II.*
Water, destruction by, 119; systems, 113
Weapons, absence of, 85, 87, 88, 94, 103, 114; Australian, 106; divine, 38; for hunting, 106; hypersonic, 20; medieval, 116; of mass destruction, 120; nuclear, 29, 120; Stone Age, 72
West Africa, 59, 77, 95, 114, 115
West, Geoffrey, 48
Wheat, awned, 8, 9, 74, 75, 76, 113; consumed by cattle, 39; and the Golden Age, 38, 74, 75; refined, 39; grown in Crete and by the Minoans, 86, 88; grown near Gobekli Tepe, 79; grown at Mehrgarh, 94, 113; grown by Yamnaya, 60; world regions grown in, 53
Whole grains, 39, *See Barley, Buckwheat, Maize, Millet, Oats, Rice, Rye, Teff, Wheat.*
Wild animals, 8, 11, 51, 59, 65, 66, 94, 99, 105, 106, 113, 119; fruit, 68; grains, 11, 38, 53, 64, 68, 70, 71, 76, 77, 79, 95, 96, 99, 105, 106, 107, 110, 112, 113, 114; grasses, 52, 63, 64, 65, 70, 71, 110, 112, 114; plants, 8, 11, 59, 70, 105, 107, 110, 114; reeds and cane, 103
Wild rice, 53, 95, 96, 110
Wilderness Era, 73, 82
Witzel, E. J. Michael, 50
Women, in Australia, 133; as author of great literature, 132; oppression of, 39; role in Minoan culture, 87, 88; subordination in Sumer, Egypt, Babylon, and Assyria, 87. *See also Divine Feminine.*
Wood, as a fuel 16; for cooking 70, 119; for cookware, 99, 110; humans created from, 100; for dwellings, 102; for musical instruments, 105; for plow, 94; for tools, 71, 105, 110; for tools by animals, 122, 123
World federal government, 120
World hunger, 129
World War I, 15, 39
World War II, 15, 21, 39, 121
Wrangham, Richard, 66
Writing, 10, 24, 41, 42, 72, 83, 98, 103, 105, 106
Wu Chen-En, 52

Yam, 95
Yamnaya, 60-61, 130
Yangtze River culture, 61
Yellow River Valley, 61
Yin and yang, of animals vs. humans, 123; of bonobos and chimps, 67; and celestial energy and precession, 42; chart of attributes, 52; definition of, 11; of grains, 123; and the two halves of the Spiral, 30-31; and the Minoan double axe, 89; and the Spiral of History, 33; symbol, 31; as the unifying principle, 52; use of by Toynbee; ways of eating, 40-41
Yoga, 120
Younger Dryas, 77, 119
Yucatan, 8
Zebu bull, 93
Zeus, 85
Zumdick, Bettina, 52

About the Author

Alex Jack is an author, teacher, and macrobiotic dietary counselor living in the Berkshires. He is founder and president of Planetary Health, Inc., a non-profit educational organization that sponsors the Amberwaves grassroots campaign to preserve whole grains from genetic engineering, climate change, and other threats; holds conferences and seminars on diet, health, and sustainability; engages in publishing; and conducts medical research.

He grew up in Evanston, Illinois and Scarsdale, New York and studied philosophy, religion, and the classics at Oberlin College, Benares Hindu University, and Boston University School of Theology. He served as a civil rights worker in Mississippi, Vietnam War correspondent, editor-in-chief of *East West Journal*, director of the One Peaceful World Society, and executive director of Kushi Institute. He serves on the guest faculty of Rosas Contemporary Dance Company in Brussels, the Kushi Institute of Europe in Amsterdam, and the Ohsawa Center in Tokyo. He has also presented at the Zen Temple in Beijing, the Cardiology Institute of St. Petersburg, and Shakespeare's New Globe Theatre in London.

His major books include *The Cancer Prevention Diet, One Peaceful World,* and *The Gospel of Peace: Jesus's Teachings of Eternal Truth* with Michio Kushi; *The Mozart Effect: Tapping the Power of Music to Heal the Body, Strengthen the Mind, and Unlock the Creative Spirit* with Don Campbell; editions and commentaries on *Hamlet* and *As You Like It* by Christopher Marlowe and William Shakespeare; and *The One Peaceful World Cookbook* with Sachi Kato.

Alex has one daughter and five grandchildren and resides on October Mountain in western Massachusetts where he directs Planetary Health, Inc. and gives personal dietary guidance and way of life consultations.

Contact: shenwa26@yahoo.com